Hiking the Upper McCullough Gulch Trail.

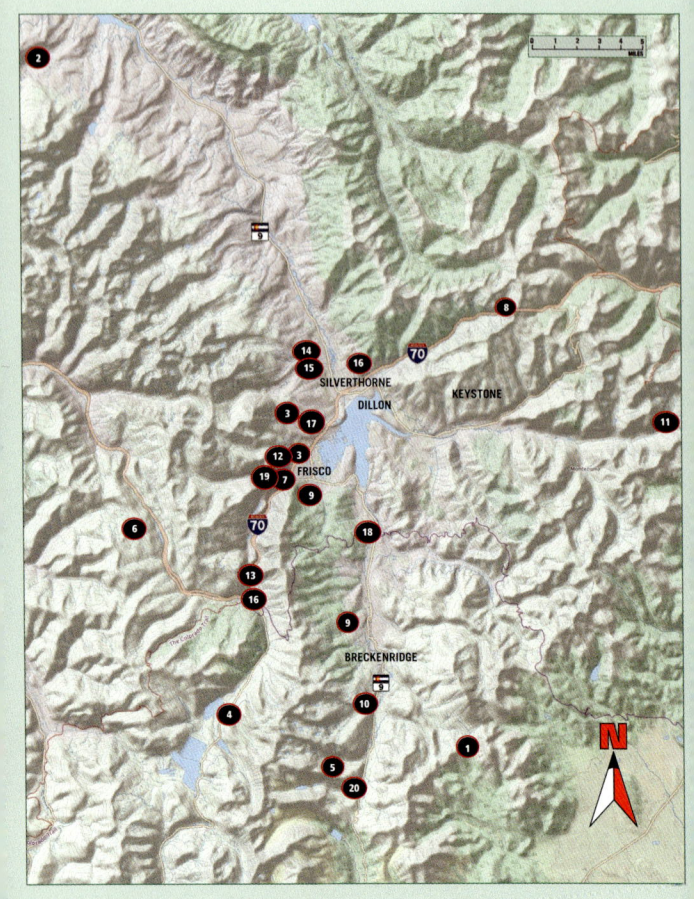

# CONTENTS

*Foreword* .................................................. 6

Using this Guide .......................................... 8
The Ten Essentials ...................................... 15

## THE HIKES

1. Black Powder Pass ........................ 16
2. Lower Cataract Lake ...................... 20
3. Lily Pad Lake ............................. 24
4. Mayflower Gulch .......................... 30
5. McCullough Gulch ......................... 34
6. Shrine Mountain .......................... 38
7. North Tenmile Creek ...................... 42
8. Continental Divide Overlook .............. 46
9. Peaks Trail .............................. 50
10. Mohawk Lakes ............................ 56
11. Argentine Pass .......................... 62
12. Eccles Pass ............................. 66
13. Uneva Pass .............................. 70
14. Red Buffalo Pass ........................ 74
15. Willow Lakes ............................ 80
16. Ptarmigan Peak .......................... 84
17. Buffalo Mountain ........................ 88
18. Colorado Trail Section 7 ................ 92
19. Peak 1 .................................. 98
20. Quandary Peak ........................... 102

About the Author .......................................... 106
Checklist ................................................. 107

# FOREWORD

When I was approached to do this book I thought it was a great idea. Like other books in the pack guide series, this guide highlights 20 of the best hikes in the area. Each hike, described in detail, is ranked by difficulty and includes up-to-date metrics, maps, and photos. A GPS track on the map clearly marks the route. Intentionally done in a concise format, use it to choose a hike and then throw it in your pack before heading out. It works for novice and experienced hikers alike.

Choosing "the best" 20 hikes in Summit County is not easy. The Dillon Ranger District of the US Forest Service lists over 80 hikes in their system. Ask 20 people and you'll get 20 different lists of the best hikes. But most of the hikes in this book would appear on those lists. For this guide I chose hikes that:

- are day hikes.
- are on well-defined trails that are generally easy to follow.
- are easy to get to (four-wheel-drive vehicles are not required).
- are on public lands.
- avoid areas where motorized vehicles are permitted.
- can be done without any technical climbing skills.
- have something special to offer.

Most hikes in this book make good snowshoe or cross-country ski routes in the winter. In a typical year, you will encounter snow on many of these trails from October to June. If you have never put on a pair of snowshoes and hiked into the forest, you're missing out. Just be extra careful with your planning and route finding.

I completed all of these hikes in the summer of 2016. The trail information and GPS tracks are up to date as of that time.

COLORADO
MOUNTAIN CLUB
PACK GUIDE

# THE BEST
# Summit
# County
# HIKES

**MARSHALL HULL**

The Colorado Mountain Club Press
Golden, Colorado

*The Best Summit County Hikes*
© 2017 by The Colorado Mountain Club

All rights reserved. No part of this publication may be reproduced or transmitted in any form or by any means, electronic or mechanical, including photocopy, recording, or by any information storage and retrieval system, without permission in writing from the publisher.

**PUBLISHED BY**

The Colorado Mountain Club Press
710 Tenth Street, Suite 200, Golden, Colorado 80401
303-996-2743
e-mail: cmcpress@cmc.org • website: http://www.cmc.org

Founded in 1912, The Colorado Mountain Club is the largest outdoor recreation, education, and conservation organization in the Rocky Mountains. Look for our books at your local bookstore or outdoor retailer or online at www.cmc.org/store.

>    Marshall Hull: Author and photographer
>    Emiko Hull: Contributor and soulmate
>    Jodi Jennings: copyeditor
>    Erika K. Arroyo: design, composition, and production
>    Clyde Soles: publisher

DISTRIBUTED TO THE BOOK TRADE BY
The Mountaineers Books, 1001 SW Klickitat Way, Suite 201,
Seattle, WA 98134, 800-553-4453, www.mountaineersbooks.org

TOPOGRAPHIC MAPS generated with CalTopo.com.

COVER PHOTO: On the way to Willow Lakes.

We gratefully acknowledge the financial support of the people of Colorado through the Scientific and Cultural Facilities District of greater Denver for our publishing activities.

**WARNING:** Although there has been an effort to make the trail descriptions in this book as accurate as possible, some discrepancies may exist between the text and the trails in the field. Hiking in mountainous and desert areas is a high-risk activity. This guidebook is not a substitute for your experience and common sense. The users of this guidebook assume full responsibility for their own safety. Weather, terrain conditions, and individual abilities must be considered before undertaking any of the hikes in this guide.

First Edition

ISBN 978-1-935052-42-3

This book is intended for trail hikers. It is not a reference for off-trail hikers, mountain bikers, rock climbers, ski mountaineers, kayakers, four-wheelers, anglers, hunters, history buffs, geologists, or botanists. There are better references for those activities. Nor does this book attempt to be a comprehensive volume of all the trails in Summit County or a historical account of those who pioneered them. There are other references for that too.

Many of the hikes on the Summit County side of the Eagles Nest Wilderness Area require long approaches and involve off-trail hiking or bushwhacking. Because of this, they are usually done as multi-day backpacking trips. A few hikes in this book can be linked together for longer, multi-day outings, and these have been noted.

When on the trail, always be considerate of others and respect the beauty and significance of the public areas you are visiting. Follow the Leave No Trace and Wilderness Area Rules (see page 12-14). Plan ahead, inform someone else of your plan, and carry the Ten Essentials (see page 15).

Hiking above Black Powder Pass.

# Using This Guide

Each hike in this book starts with a summary of the hike metrics. Difficulty ratings and time estimates will vary depending on the person.

The RATING is a relative measure as compared to other hikes in this book. A moderate hike may be too much for some and too easy for others. Each rating is based mainly on three factors: trail quality, distance, and elevation gain. If you're not sure which level is appropriate for you, start with an easy hike and move up from there. You can always turn around.

ROUND TRIP DISTANCE is the total distance covered by the hike in miles. For an out-and-back hike, the round-trip distance is given. For a thru-hike (point-to-point) the total distance is given.

The ROUND TRIP TIME estimate is the approximate time required to complete the entire hike (there and

Western Yellow Paintbrush and Elephant's Head near Eccles Pass.

back). A common rule of thumb is to assume 1 hour for each 2 miles of distance plus another hour for each 1,000 feet of elevation gain, not including breaks. For experienced hikers, this will seem slow. The times in this book are based on my experience hiking at a reasonable pace with a reasonable amount of time for breaks. Don't assume you can complete the hike in the estimated time until you have some sense of your own pace.

ELEVATION GAIN is the total uphill hiking one way. This is not the net elevation gain. For example, hiking up 1,200 feet to a ridge, then down 300 feet into a small valley, and then up another 400 feet to your destination, the total elevation climbed is 1,600 feet, not 1,300 feet.

The TRAILHEAD name, altitude, and Universal Transverse Mercator (UTM) coordinates are also listed. The UTM coordinates are in WGS84.

The MAPS section shows the standard National Geographic Trails Illustrated map(s) and USGS 7.5 minute quadrangle map(s) covering the hike. Each hike in this book includes a color topographical map with a GPS track of the route. Consider taking a more detailed map with you, particularly for the moderate and difficult hikes. Note that trail locations on Trails Illustrated and USGS maps are sometimes outdated and inaccurate. The GPS tracks in this book are up to date and accurate to within a few feet.

The NEAREST LANDMARK is also noted. This is usually the nearest township.

An OPTIONS section suggests popular alternatives for some routes, which are worth the extra effort. Some options add mileage, elevation, and time, which are indicated. Some options shorten the route and make for an easier hike. Either way, that information is not factored into the hike rating.

## GET THE TRACKS

If you would like the GPS data for a hike in this book, email me at summitcountyhikes@gmail.com. I will email you a gpx file that can be imported into the gadget of your choice. Please do not ask for all of the hikes. And don't wait until the last minute—I might be out on a hike.

Also feel free to let me know what you think about this pack guide. Suggestions for improvements to this guide are always welcome.

## SUMMIT COUNTY CLIMATE

Summit County is covered in snow more often than not. Many of the hikes in this book make good snowshoe and cross-county ski routes. However, following these trails is much more difficult when they are covered with snow. Take extra precautions for winter travel and be sure to follow your progress on a map. Snow-covered trails often start off packed down and easy to follow but become less traveled and more difficult to find. Turn around when you are not comfortable. Always avoid areas of avalanche danger.

Expect to encounter snow on many of these hikes well into June, and July at higher elevations. Snow tends to linger on north-facing aspects, especially in shaded areas.

During the summer months, mornings are typically clear and calm and afternoons are turbulent and stormy. The best time to hike is almost always early in the morning. Get an early start—you'll be glad you did.

Elevation gain can change your comfort level dramatically. Winds are often stronger up high and usually much colder, especially above treeline. Carry extra layers, gloves, and a hat that covers your ears.

The sun's radiation is more intense at higher elevations. Always protect your skin.

I recommend a good pair of waterproof hiking boots, especially on the moderate and difficult hikes in this guide. Many trails have stream crossings, most of which have wooden bridges, but a wet foot on a long hike is not comfortable. Generally speaking, running shoes or sneakers are not recommended.

## ALTITUDE SICKNESS

Is altitude sickness an issue for you? Almost all of the hikes in this book go above treeline. In Summit County, treeline is around 11,500 feet. If you are visiting Summit County from a lower elevation, give yourself a few days to adjust before heading up.

## WILD ANIMALS

On many of the hikes in this book, you may encounter wild animals like mountain goats, moose, elk, deer, marmots, and possibly bears. Never approach or feed wild animals. If you encounter a wild animal, raise your arms and walk backward slowly. Dogs should always be on a leash.

For more information visit www.cpw.state.co.us

## WILDFLOWERS

Peak wildflower season is generally late June to mid-August for most of the hikes in this book. This changes somewhat depending on the altitude and the aspect of the terrain. Lower elevations peak earlier.

For more information visit www.nps.gov/romo/learn/nature/wildflowers.htm.

## DILLON RANGER DISTRICT

Almost all of the trails in this book are under the purview of the Dillon Ranger District, which is part of the US Forest Service. The district has an excellent public information center in Silverthorne, staffed with friendly people willing to answer your questions. They can help with camping and fishing information and they also sell maps.

Dillon Ranger District (970) 468-5400
680 Blue River Parkway
Silverthorne, CO 80498

For more information visit www.fs.usda.gov/recarea/whiteriver/recreation/hiking/recarea/?recid=40417

## SUMMIT COUNTY RECREATION PATH SYSTEM

Summit County has a paved recreation path system (the "rec path"). While none of the hikes in this book are focused on the rec path, any section of the rec path can make for a good walk. The rec path is extensive and well maintained and is wheelchair accessible in many places. Be sure to follow rec path rules and always be aware of cyclists.

The posted rec path rules are:

- Obey all traffic signs, signals, and pavement markings.
- Travel at a reasonable and safe speed, never faster than 25 miles per hour.
- Signal other users before passing them.
- Control dogs by 6-foot leash at all times. Remove pet waste.
- Step off of the pathway when stopping. Do not stop on or obstruct the pathway.
- Travel on the right side unless you are passing others.
- Pass only when the pathway is clear and unobstructed by other users.
- Motorized vehicles, including electric bikes, are prohibited on the pathway except where posted.
- In the event of an emergency, call 911.

For more information visit www.co.summit.co.us/DocumentCenter/Home/View/910

## HIKING IN WILDERNESS AREAS

Established by the 1964 Wilderness Act, wilderness areas are federal lands designated by Congress as part of the National Wilderness Preservation System. These are special places that

Wilderness Area sign at Lower Cataract Falls.

have been put aside to preserve their natural state and minimize the impact of human activity. There are two wilderness areas in Summit County: Eagles Nest Wilderness Area and Ptarmigan Wilderness Area. This is a partial list of the rules that apply to all visitors in wilderness areas:

- No motorized vehicles or mechanized equipment are permitted.
- Dogs must be on a leash at all times.
- Camping is prohibited within 100 feet of all lakes, streams, and trails.
- Fires are not permitted above treeline, in meadows, or within 100 feet of streams or trails.
- Fires are not permitted within 0.25 mile of lakes.
- Practice "Leave No Trace" principles.

For more information visit www.wilderness.net

## LEAVE NO TRACE

These basic, common sense principles were established to promote ethical behavior and respect for nature and others while hiking in the backcountry.

- Plan Ahead and Prepare.
- Travel and Camp on Durable Surfaces.
- Dispose of Waste Properly.
- Leave What You Find.
- Minimize Campfire Impacts.
- Respect Wildlife.
- Be Considerate of Other Visitors.

When hiking on a trail, stay on the trail as much as possible. Don't cut switchbacks.

For more information: www.lnt.org

Mayflower Gulch.

# The Ten Essentials

The ten essentials is a standardized list of what you should always carry into the wilderness. For most of the hikes in this book, all of these items may not be necessary. For longer off-trail hikes and backpack trips, they definitely are.

1. Navigation: map, compass, altimeter, GPS.
2. Sun Protection: sunscreen, sunglasses, lip balm, cap.
3. Insulation: rain gear, down jacket, gloves, ear protection.
4. Illumination: headlamp, small flashlight.
5. First-aid: gauze, bandages, painkiller, moleskin, bug spray.
6. Fire: matches, lighter.
7. Repair kit: knife.
8. Extra Food.
9. Extra Water.
10. Emergency overnight protection.

Let someone know where you're going, when to expect you back and what to do if you're overdue. Always know where you are on the map. Plan ahead and prepare. Most of these hikes travel outside cellphone range.

Mountain Goat on Buffalo Mountain.

# 1. Black Powder Pass

| | |
|---|---|
| **RATING** | Easy |
| **ROUND-TRIP DISTANCE** | 2.8 miles |
| **ROUND-TRIP TIME** | 2.0 hours |
| **ELEVATION GAIN** | 700 feet |
| **TRAILHEAD** | Black Powder Pass Trailhead at Boreas Pass (11,496 feet) (13S 0416662E 4362788N) |
| **MAPS** | Trails Illustrated 108 Vail, Frisco, Dillon; USGS Boreas Pass Quadrangle |
| **NEAREST LANDMARK** | Breckenridge |
| **OPTIONS** | Additional short hike up to French Pass overlook |

**OVERVIEW:** Southeast of Breckenridge, this short hike starts at 11,490 feet on Boreas Pass, right on the Continental Divide. The trail leads up to 12,159-foot Black Powder Pass, a saddle on the ridgeline between Boreas Mountain (13,082 feet) to the south and Bald Mountain (13,684 feet) to the north. Views from the pass include the southern Tenmile Range and the peaks along the Continental Divide to the south. The combination of a mellow route and beautiful views make this hike very popular with families and dog owners. The trail has recently been improved and is easy to follow.

Once known as Breckenridge Pass, from 1872 to 1938 Boreas Pass was used as a narrow-gauge railroad route that linked Park and Summit counties. Information kiosks near the trailhead describe some of the history of this area. Two of the original buildings from that time, Section House and Ken's Cabin, have been restored and are now operated as winter cabins for backcountry skiers.

The drive from Breckenridge up to Boreas Pass is also noteworthy. Most of the road is not paved and is narrow in spots. But the scenery is beautiful and there are several historic sites along the way, for example, Bakers Tank, a restored railroad water tower 6.6 miles from Highway 9. Much of the road winds through aspen forest, making it a very popular drive in the fall. Expect the road to be crowded in late September.

**GETTING THERE:** From the intersection of Highway 9 and Boreas Pass Road on the south side of Breckenridge, go east on Boreas Pass Road. Follow the road for about 9.6 miles up to Boreas Pass. You will see an old railroad car and two restored buildings at the pass. Look for parking on either side of the road. The trailhead is on the east side of the road. This parking area is not large and fills up quickly on weekends, especially in the fall. Park along the road if necessary. There is no fee to park here. There are no restroom facilities.

Boreas Pass Road is closed to motorized vehicles during the winter at a gate about 3.5 miles from Highway 9. This gate, at 10,360 feet, is the winter trailhead for snowshoeing and backcountry ski tours. Hiking the snow-covered road 6 miles up to the pass makes for a long day. Note that this area is also open to snowmobiles.

**THE ROUTE:** Find the Black Powder Pass Trailhead sign on the east side of the road, in front of and to the left of Section House. Follow the trail north and then east up through an open meadow as it runs along an old canal ditch (Boreas Ditch #2). At about 0.1 mile, pass a small canal gate on your left. Continue into a short section of trees and cross a bridge over a wet area to emerge on a high meadow. From here, the trail follows a shallow drainage line northeast toward the pass. Wildflowers along this section of the trail are plentiful in the summer, especially along the water. The remaining route up to the pass is obvious. Follow it another 0.6 mile and 560 feet up. At 1.4 miles, reach Black Powder Pass.

Boreas Pass and the Section House

At Black Powder Pass, you are again standing on the Continental Divide as well as the border between Summit and Park counties. Park County is directly to the east. To the north along the divide is Bald Mountain (13,684 feet), and to the south is Boreas Mountain (13,082 feet). To the southwest, Red Peak is in the foreground (not the Red Peak near Buffalo Mountain), and looming large behind it, in Park County, is Mount Silverheels (13,822 feet). Directly west, across the Blue River Valley, is the south end of the Tenmile Range. Quandary Peak is the highpoint at 14,265 feet. Mountain goats are sometimes seen on Black Powder Pass. To return to the parking area, reverse your route.

## OPTIONS

**French Pass Overlook:** Additional round-trip: 0.8 miles; 315 feet up.

If you still have energy and the weather is holding, follow the ridgeline north, up toward Bald Mountain. Start by working your way around the big rock outcrop. The trail is faint at times, but if you stay on the ridge you will reach a flat area on the ridge at 12,538 feet that offers views not available from Black Powder Pass. French Pass, connecting Bald Mountain and Mt. Guyot, is visible down to the north. Mt. Guyot (13,370 feet) is the peak just above French Pass.

BLACK POWDER PASS

# 2. Lower Cataract Lake

| | |
|---|---|
| **RATING** | Easy |
| **ROUND-TRIP DISTANCE** | 2.3 miles |
| **ROUND-TRIP TIME** | 2.0 hours |
| **ELEVATION GAIN** | 200 feet |
| **TRAILHEAD** | Lower Cataract Lake Trailhead (8,658 feet) (13S 0387403E 4410532N) |
| **MAPS** | Trails Illustrated 149 Eagles Nest, Holy Cross Wilderness Areas; USGS Mount Powell Quadrangle |
| **NEAREST LANDMARK** | Silverthorne |

**OVERVIEW:** This popular Summit County hike follows a short loop trail around Lower Cataract Lake in the Eagles Nest Wilderness Area. The trail is very pleasant and passes through a variety of ecosystems as it follows the lake's shoreline. On the west end of the lake, a waterfall cascades down from the drainage basin north of Eagles Nest Peak (13,432 feet), the top of which is visible from the east end of the lake. Waterfowl, beavers, and muskrats are often seen along the way. This hike is also excellent for summer wildflowers and fall colors (mid- to late September). It is a good choice for families and those that are looking for an easy half-day hike.

This trail can be busy on weekends and is popular with dog owners. Always follow the wilderness area rules and keep your dog on a leash.

Cataract Creek Road is not plowed during the winter months, which makes this area difficult to reach.

**GETTING THERE:** From Interstate 70 exit 205 in Silverthorne, head north on Highway 9 for approximately 16.6 miles and watch carefully for the Heeney Road sign. Turn left onto Heeney Road and follow it around Green Mountain

Eagles Nest Peak above Lower Cataract Lake.

Reservoir for 5.5 miles where you will take a sharp left onto Cataract Creek Road 1725. Follow this narrow dirt road for 2.6 miles, past the Surprise Lake Trailhead, to a large parking area at the end of the road. The road is gated at this point; do not block the gate. There is no parking fee. There is a restroom.

**THE ROUTE:** Find the trailhead at the west end of the parking area, near the restroom. Because the trail is just a big loop around the lake, the hike can be done in a clockwise or counterclockwise direction. Described clockwise, take the left-most trail to the south (not the middle one directly toward the lake). Head out across the meadow and just before you reach the east end of the lake, cross Cataract Creek on a stout wooden bride. At 0.2 mile (8,635 feet) pass the Eagles Nest Wilderness boundary sign. Continue through an open sagebrush meadow along the south side of the lake. Look for wildlife in a small pond next to the lake. This area is flush with wildflowers in the summer, including a hillside full of columbine.

Lower Cataract Lake and the Williams Fork Range.

At the west end of the lake the trail enters dense forest as it approaches the falls. At 1.1 miles (8,681 feet), cross a long wooden bridge over the creek at the bottom of the falls. The falls is not visible from here but definitely can be heard. Note that social trails up along the waterfalls can be steep and hazardous. Shortly after this, the trail turns north and wraps around the west end of the lake as it leaves the forest and enters an open meadow. Trout can often be seen in the shallow waters of the creek as it flows into the west end of the lake. Across the meadow the trail climbs gradually over 100 feet above the north side of the lake and winds through an aspen grove. Look back along this section for better views of the falls and Eagles Nest Peak (13,432 feet). Continue east along the north side of the lake and at 1.7 miles (8,727 feet) pass a wooden gate and leave the Eagles Nest Wilderness Area. At 2.1 miles (8,6/8 feet) the trail empties onto a dirt road. Follow the dirt road east another 0.2 mile back to the trailhead and parking area.

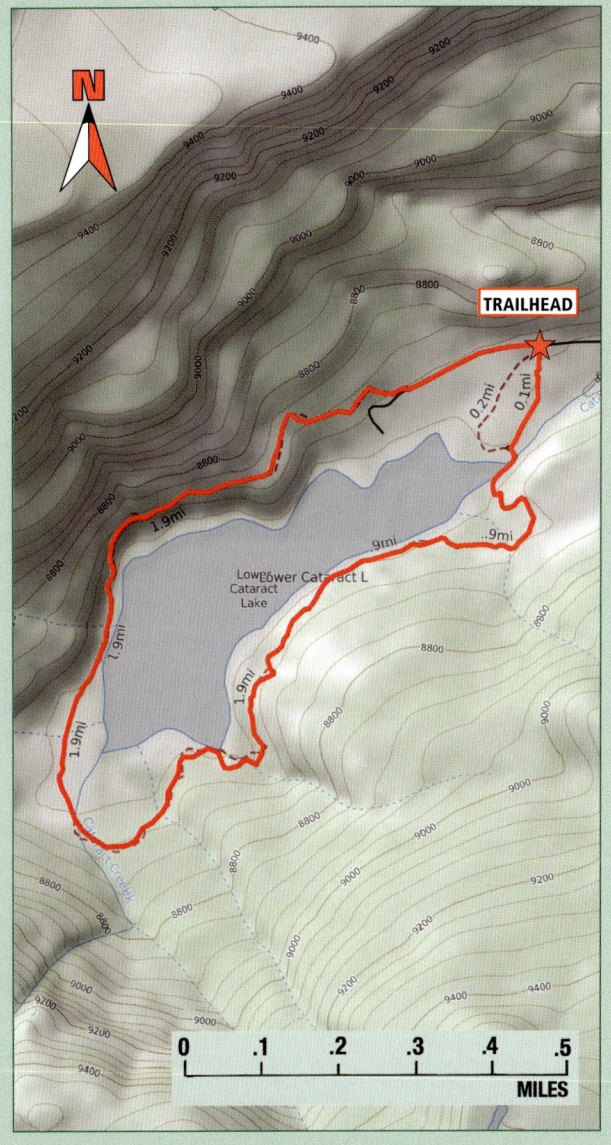

LOWER CATARACT LAKE

# 3. Lily Pad Lake

| | |
|---|---|
| **RATING** | Easy |
| **ROUND-TRIP DISTANCE** | 3.2 miles (from Lily Pad Lake Trailhead) <br> 3.2 miles (from Meadow Creek Trailhead) |
| **ROUND-TRIP TIME** | 3.0 hours (from Lily Pad Lake Trailhead) <br> 3.5 hours (from Meadow Creek Trailhead) |
| **ELEVATION GAIN** | 284 feet (from Lily Pad Lake Trailhead) <br> 806 feet (from Meadow Creek Trailhead) |
| **TRAILHEAD** | Lily Pad Lake Trailhead (9,806 feet) (13S 0404681E 4386062N) <br> Meadow Creek Trailhead (9,160 feet) (13S 0405030E 4382728N) |
| **MAPS** | Trails Illustrated 108 Vail, Frisco, Dillon; USGS Frisco Quadrangle |
| **NEAREST LANDMARK** | Silverthorne (Lily Pad Lake Trailhead) <br> Frisco (Meadow Creek Trailhead) |
| **OPTIONS** | Hike from Lily Pad Lake Trailhead to Meadow Creek Trailhead. Requires a car shuttle. |

**OVERVIEW:** This popular hike takes you to a pair of picturesque lakes in the forest of the Eagles Nest Wilderness Area. The lakes can be accessed from two different trailheads: the Lily Pad Lakes Trailhead in Silverthorne or the Meadow Creek Trailhead in Frisco. The distance covered from either trailhead is about the same but hiking from Frisco requires more elevation gain. For a slightly longer outing, hike from one trailhead to the other, passing the lakes along the way (see OPTIONS). Easy trailhead access and well-marked trails make this a perfect route for a family or someone

Lily Pad Lake.

who wants to get in half a day of easy hiking on a mellow trail. This trail also makes a good winter route. Moose are sometimes encountered in this area.

**GETTING THERE:** Lily Pad Lake Trailhead: Parking for Lily Pad Lake is the same as parking for Buffalo Mountain (Hike 17). The trailhead is not the same. The Lily Pad Lake Trailhead is at the south end of the parking area.

Meadow Creek Trailhead: Parking for Lily Pad Lake is the same as parking for Eccles Pass (Hike 12). Use the same trailhead (Meadow Creek).

**THE ROUTE (FROM LILY PAD LAKE TRAILHEAD):** Find the Lily Pad Lake Trailhead sign around the bend at the south end of the parking area. Note that this parking area services two trailheads: Lily Pad Lake and Buffalo Mountain. The trailheads are at opposite ends of the parking area, and both are well marked. Head due south from the trailhead up a dirt road that doubles as the start of the trail. Stay to the right (west) of a fenced-in area and pick up the trail as it enters a small meadow. You should be looking directly south at Peak 1

Lily Pad Lake.

(12,805 feet) in the distance, with Buffalo Mountain (12,777 feet) looming large to your right (west). In the distance to your left (east) is a good view of Dillon Reservoir and the Continental Divide. Fourteeners Grays Peak (14,270 feet) and Torreys Peak (14,267 feet) mark the high points on the horizon. Continue south on this easy trail as it enters lodgepole pine forest.

At 0.3 mile enter the Eagles Nest Wilderness Area. Be sure to follow all rules regarding hiking in US Forest Service wilderness areas. Soon after this point, cross the first of several wooden bridges. Even though this hike is relatively short, it's a good idea to wear waterproof footwear, especially in the early summer. At about 0.7 mile, just after crossing a small boulder field, the trail is somewhat confusing. Look for a sign confirming the way and be cautious with your route finding. At 1.1 miles pass the Salt Lick Trail junction on your left. Continue to the right on the Lily Pad Lake Trail. At 1.5 miles arrive at Lily Pad Lake.

**THE ROUTE (FROM MEADOW CREEK TRAILHEAD):** Find the obvious Meadow Creek Trail sign and kiosk on the north side of the parking area. Follow the trail north and then west as

Lily Pad Lake and Peak One.

it climbs first through tall aspen and then lodgepole pine forests. At 0.5 mile, pass the remains of an old log cabin on your left and then at 0.6 mile, reach the trail junction sign to Lily Pad Lakes. Go right onto the Lily Pad Lake Trail and follow the trail up to the north. At 0.9 mile cross Meadow

On the Lily Pad Lake trail.

Creek on a stout wooden bridge and enter the Eagles Nest Wilderness Area. A small waterfall is just above this crossing. Shortly after this, pass through a small clearing with views to the southeast of Frisco. Bald Mountain (13,684 feet) and Mt. Guyot (13,370 feet) are in the distance. At 1.6 miles (9,915 feet), reach Lily Pad Lake.

**THE ROUTE (THE LAKES):** There are two lakes, and the trail goes between them. The smaller lake on the east side of the trail has more lily pads. The larger lake on the west side of the trail does not have many lily pads but is more picturesque. Mid- to late July is a good time to see the lily pads blooming. Regardless of the time of year, this is an excellent area to take a break and enjoy the peace and quiet of the wilderness area. Guard your lunch from aggressive chipmunks. Reverse your route to return to the parking area.

## OPTIONS
You may want to hike from one trailhead to the other. It will require a car shuttle as you will end up over 3 miles from where you started.

### LILY PAD LAKE TRAILHEAD TO MEADOW CREEK TRAILHEAD
Total one-way travel: 3.1 miles; 336 feet up, 984 feet down

LILY PAD LAKE

# 4. Mayflower Gulch

| | |
|---|---|
| **RATING** | Easy |
| **ROUND-TRIP DISTANCE** | 3.0 miles |
| **ROUND-TRIP TIME** | 3 hours |
| **ELEVATION GAIN** | 594 feet |
| **TRAILHEAD** | Mayflower Gulch Trailhead (10,987 feet) (13S 0399710E 4365164N) |
| **MAPS** | Trails Illustrated 109 Breckenridge, Tennessee Pass; USGS Copper Mountain Quadrangle |
| **NEAREST LANDMARK** | Copper Mountain |
| **OPTIONS** | Additional hike to Upper Mines (12,383 feet) |

**OVERVIEW:** Just south of Copper Mountain, Mayflower Gulch is a Summit County classic. This hike follows a short mining road along Mayflower Creek to a beautiful alpine meadow just above treeline. The meadow sits at the base of a dramatic sawtooth ridge along the west side of the Tenmile Range. The ridge and its surrounding peaks form a spectacular natural amphitheater at the head of the gulch. Impressive views and prolific wildflowers create an ideal alpine mountain experience. Ruins from an old mining settlement, including log cabins, still remain here. This trail is popular year-round and makes an excellent entry-level snowshoe and crosscountry ski area in the winter.

**GETTING THERE:** Take Interstate 70 to the Copper Mountain exit (195). Follow Highway 91 south toward Leadville for 5.3 miles. Turn left (east) into a large unmarked but obvious parking area beside the highway. This is the Mayflower Gulch Trailhead parking area. There is no fee to park here. There are no restrooms.

Mayflower Gulch.

It is possible to drive the road to the cabins in the summer. There are no designated parking places at the cabins, so this is recommended only for those physically unable to do the hike from the trailhead (1.5 miles).

**THE ROUTE:** Find the trailhead sign at the southeast end of the parking area. Go past the sign and follow the dirt road southeast as it climbs gradually up Mayflower Gulch. Mayflower Creek is down to your left (north). At about 0.2 mile, you will reach a fork in the road. A water diversion gate is on the left fork. Stay on the right fork and continue southeast up through the forest. At 0.75 mile, pass the remains of an old cabin on your left. Just past this cabin, pass the remains of a wooden mining chute on your right.

At 1.5 miles (11,524 feet) you will come to an opening in the trees and a fork in the road. The fork to the right takes you up to Gold Hill. Stay left toward the cabins, which are just up ahead. Pass a gate on the road and continue up to the cabins at 1.5 miles (11,550 feet). As you hike up to the cabins, the meadow at the top of Mayflower Gulch opens up

Mining cabin in Mayflower Gulch.

and you will immediately understand why this hike is so popular. Pick a spot to take a break and take it all in.

The log cabins are part of what was a settlement for gold mining operations during the late 1800s and early 1900s. Mayflower Creek and the surrounding meadow provide fantastic wildflower viewing in the summer months. The headwall of the gulch is anchored on the left by Atlantic Peak (13,841 feet); Fletcher Mountain (13,951 feet) is set back in the middle; and Drift Peak (13,900 feet) is on the right. Atlantic and Fletcher are two of the highest 100 peaks in the state, known as "the Centennial Peaks." The jagged ridge connecting them is unofficially known as Rockfountain Ridge. To the west, framed by the valley and neighbor to Copper Mountain Ski Area, is Jacque Peak (13,205 feet).

Reverse your route to return to the parking area. Or take the extra hike up to the mines (see Options).

## OPTIONS

**UPPER MINES:** Additional round-trip: 2.4 miles; 856 feet up.

To hike up to the mines, continue southeast along the trail past the cabins as it winds up through the meadow. At 2.7 miles (11,925 feet) you will reach a gate. Follow the trail past the gate and east as it switchbacks up an old rocky access road. At 2.9 miles (12,383 feet) the road levels out in front of two old mineshafts. Obey the posted signs and do not attempt to enter the mines. There is a wooden bench near the first mine that makes a good place to take a break and enjoy the views. From here, it is 2.7 miles back to the trailhead parking area.

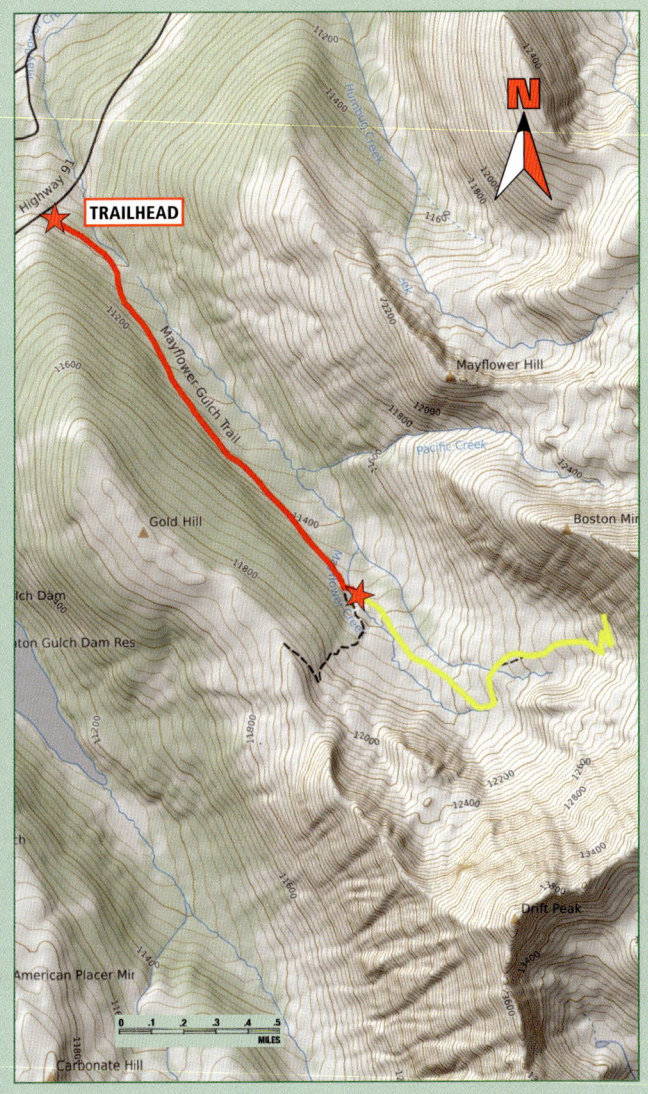

# 5. McCullough Gulch

| | |
|---|---|
| **RATING** | Easy-Moderate |
| **ROUND-TRIP DISTANCE** | 2.8 miles |
| **ROUND-TRIP TIME** | 3.0 hours |
| **ELEVATION GAIN** | 918 feet |
| **TRAILHEAD** | McCullough Gulch Trailhead (11,100 feet)  13S 0407069E 4361841N |
| **MAPS** | Trails Illustrated 109 Breckenridge, Tennessee Pass; USGS Breckenridge Quadrangle |
| **NEAREST LANDMARK** | Breckenridge |
| **OPTIONS** | Upper McCullough Gulch (12,600 feet) |

**OVERVIEW:** McCullough Gulch is the broad valley immediately north of Quandary Peak (14,265 feet). This hike follows an old mining road and trail through dense forest as it climbs up the valley. Along the way you will pass White Falls before climbing steeply up to Upper Blue Reservoir. Much of the trail is along the McCullough Gulch Creek. This is an easier moderate hike that makes a good half-day outing. For a full day, tack on the more strenuous Upper McCullough Gulch Trail. Much less traveled, Upper McCullough Gulch is open meadow terrain with impressive views of alpine lakes and peaks (see OPTIONS).

During winter, McCullough Gulch Road is closed, so it's an extra 2.2 miles each way to the McCullough Gulch Trailhead. Winter parking is at overflow parking area for Quandary Peak (see GETTING THERE).

**GETTING THERE:** From the intersection of Highway 9 and Boreas Pass Road on the south side of Breckenridge, head south on Highway 9 for about 7.3 miles, through the town of Blue

River. Look for the street sign and turn right on Blue Lakes Road (FDR 850). You will see a big parking area on your right. This is the overflow parking area for Quandary Peak Trail. Go past this parking area and immediately turn right on McCullough Gulch Road (FDR 851). Follow McCullough Gulch Road, a well-maintained dirt road, for 2.2 miles to the trailhead, where the road is gated. You will pass a fork in the road before you reach the gate; stay left. This parking area is small. Park along the road if necessary. Do not block the gate. There is no fee to park here. There are no restroom facilities.

Road to the McCullough Gulch Trailhead.

**THE ROUTE:** Find the trailhead near the kiosk and follow the dirt road southwest as it climbs up into the trees. At 0.1 mile, cross McCullough Gulch Creek on a metal bridge. The trail now heads generally northwest as it climbs through mixed conifer forest, with the enormous north face of Quandary Peak on your left. At 0.3 mile, pass an old mining site (junk yard) on your left. At 0.5 mile the trail leaves the road and continues to the left. Shortly after this point, the trail crosses a boulder field as it continues up. Follow the trail carefully through this section and look for trail signs with arrows indicating the route. At about 1.0 mile, you will reach the bottom of White Falls (11,570 feet). There are several spots to get close to the falls, but use caution, especially with children. Large flat rocks in this area make a good place to take

White Falls in McCullough Gulch.

a break and enjoy the falls. For many, this will be the day's destination.

The main trail continues up from here. Follow it carefully and avoid the many sidetracks back over to the falls. Climb steeper mixed trail and slab as you approach the top of the falls. At 1.5 miles (11,920 feet) pop out above the falls and reach the east end of Upper Blue Reservoir. The trail levels off and drops slightly down to the lakeside. Take a well-earned break near the lake and enjoy the views. If you look due west, above the low point on the ridge, you can see the summit of Fletcher Mountain (13,951 feet), one of the 100 highest peaks in Colorado. To return to the trailhead and the parking area, reverse your route.

## OPTIONS

**UPPER MCCULLOUGH GULCH TRAIL:** Additional round-trip: 2.2 miles; 660 feet up.

For the more adventurous, continue past Upper Blue Reservoir and climb the rock wall to Upper McCullough Gulch Trail. Entirely above treeline, this trail heads west across alpine tundra to an unnamed lake at 12,560 feet, offering dramatic views in all directions. Fletcher Mountain (13,951 feet) sits at the south end of the sawtooth ridge atop the valley headwall. Over this ridge is Mayflower Gulch (Hike 4). In the summer months, wildflowers flourish along the creek flowing down from the lake. This hike is well worth the extra effort, but note that the trail is less traveled and not as easy to follow. Get an early start if you plan to do this one. To return to the parking area, reverse your route.

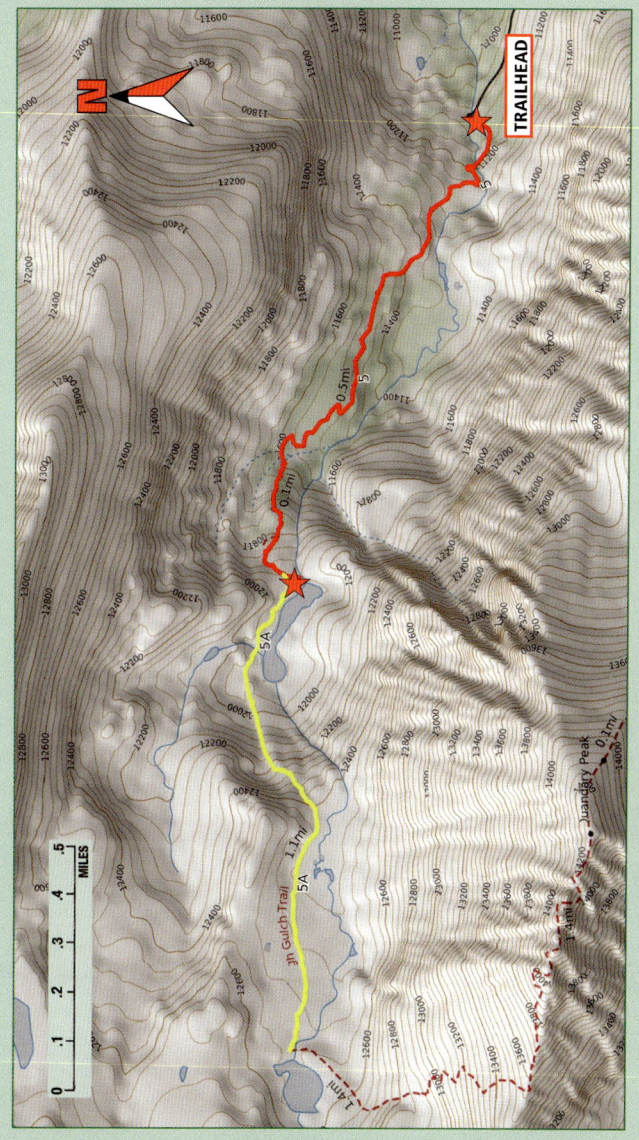

MCCULLOUGH GULCH

# 6. Shrine Mountain

| RATING | Easy-Moderate |
|---|---|
| ROUND-TRIP DISTANCE | 4.2 miles |
| ROUND-TRIP TIME | 3.0 hours |
| ELEVATION GAIN | 860 feet |
| TRAILHEAD | Shrine Mountain Trailhead (11,100 feet) (13S 0393326E 4378101N) |
| MAPS | Trails Illustrated 108 Vail, Frisco, Dillon; USGS Vail Pass, USGS Red Cliff Quadrangles |
| NEAREST LANDMARK | Vail Pass |
| OPTIONS | Additional hike along the ridge |

**OVERVIEW:** This may be the most popular hike in this book. This easy (to moderate) hike starts at 11,100 feet on Shrine Pass and follows a well-traveled trail up to the summit of Shrine Mountain at 11,888 feet. From the top of Shrine Mountain there are spectacular mountain views in all directions. The name Shrine Mountain refers to its views to the west of the Holy Cross Wilderness Area. No other hike in this guide has more comprehensive views of the southern Gore Range. This is also one of the best wildflower hikes in this guide. Be sure to take your camera.

**GETTING THERE:** Take the Vail Pass Rest Area exit (190) off Interstate 70. Head west off the exit and immediately get on Shrine Pass Road. Follow Shrine Pass Road for 2.3 miles to the trailhead parking area on the left (west) side of the road. Look for the obvious restroom building. This is a large parking area, but due to the popularity of this hike, it may fill up. Go early. There is no fee to park here. There are restrooms.

This hike is not recommended for casual winter recreation. Part of the Vail Pass Winter Recreation Area, a fee is

Gore Range from the Shrine Mountain Trail.

required to use this area in the winter months and Shrine Pass Road is not open to traffic. There is also avalanche risk on steeper terrain. Research the Vail Pass Winter Recreation Area for valuable information.

Note that Shrine Mountain Inn is a group of three privately owned cabins near Shrine Pass. Open year-round, these huts are especially popular with backcountry skiers in the winter months. For more information, see the 10th Mountain Division Hut Association website, www.huts.org.

**THE ROUTE:** This hike starts at 11,100 feet on Shrine Pass. Find the obvious trailhead on the southeast end of the parking area, next to the restrooms. Follow the dirt road for about 100 paces to the Shrine Mountain Inn gate. Go left onto the well-worn trail and follow it south as it drops down into an open, willow bush meadow. This section of the trail stays wet and marshy early in the summer. The Tenmile Range is visible in the distance to the southeast. Pacific Peak (13,950 feet) is the obvious pyramid midway, with Quandary Peak (14,265 feet) (Hike 20) looming over its south shoulder.

At 0.6 mile, the trail leaves the meadow and gradually climbs into a sparse conifer forest. At 0.9 mile (11,290 feet), you will pass a marked trail to Shrine Mountain Inn on your

Gore Range from Shrine Mountain.

right. Continue straight on the Shrine Mountain Trail through the trees. At 1.4 miles, the trail breaks out of the forest and turns to the northwest. Follow the trail along the bottom of a rocky hillside and then west as it climbs up to an obvious saddle in the ridge at 1.7 miles (11,732 feet). At this ridge you cross into Eagle County. Note that you may encounter snow here even in July. Views of the Holy Cross Wilderness with Mount of the Holy Cross (14,005 feet) are to the southwest. The snow-filled cross couloir usually remains visible well into the summer. Mt. Elbert (14,433 feet), the highest point in Colorado, and Mt. Massive (14,421 feet) are visible far to the south in the Sawatch Range.

From this point, go sharp right and follow the trail northwest up the ridgeline. The trail is braided in this area and can be confusing. Obey trail closure signs and stay on the ridgeline as it climbs gradually to the top. At 2.1 miles (11,888 feet) reach the top of Shrine Mountain. Look for the US Geological Survey marker mounted on a rock close to the ground.

Enjoy the views. Directly north is a panorama of the southern Gore Range. Mt. Powell (13,586 feet), the highest peak in the Gore Range, is visible to the left in the distance and Mt. Silverthorne (13,357 feet), the third highest peak, is closer on the right. To the east is the entire Tenmile Range. Find a good place to take a long break (see OPTIONS) and take it all in.

To return to the parking area, reverse your route.

## OPTIONS

**CONTINUE ALONG THE RIDGE:** Additional round-trip: 0.4 miles.

Continue from the top of Shrine Mountain north along the ridge trail to better places for a break. This extra hike is only 0.2 miles but the views are even better and this area tends to be less crowded

SHRINE MOUNTAIN

# 7. North Tenmile Creek

| | |
|---|---|
| **RATING** | Easy-Moderate |
| **ROUND-TRIP DISTANCE** | 6.8 miles |
| **ROUND-TRIP TIME** | 3.0 hours |
| **ELEVATION GAIN** | 918 feet |
| **TRAILHEAD** | North Tenmile Trailhead (9,160 feet) (13S 0404308E 4381280N) |
| **MAPS** | Trails Illustrated 108 Vail, Frisco, Dillon; USGS Frisco, USGS Vail Pass Quadrangles |
| **NEAREST LANDMARK** | Frisco |
| **OPTIONS** | North Tenmile Creek Trailhead to Meadow Creek Trailhead<br>North Tenmile Creek Trailhead to Copper Mountain |

**OVERVIEW:** This hike starts in Frisco and heads west along North Tenmile Creek into the Eagles Nest Wilderness Area. The trail climbs gradually over old mining access through dense forest between Wichita Mountain (10,855 feet) and Chief Mountain (11,377 feet). Along the way it passes beaver ponds and wooded meadows. Moose are sometimes seen in this area. The hike described here ends where the North Tenmile Creek Trail meets the Gore Range Trail, about 3.4 miles from the North Tenmile Creek Trailhead. Because this trail enters the wilderness area, motorized vehicles and bicycles are not allowed. This trail is very popular with dog owners and makes a great snowshoe or ski route in the winter. Never snowshoed? Give this one a try.

The North Tenmile Creek Trail is often used as one leg of a longer hike. See OPTIONS below for two excellent loop hikes.

**GETTING THERE:** Parking for this hike is at the west end of Main Street in Frisco, immediately west of Interstate 70 exit 201.

Hiking the North Tenmile Creek Trail.

Don't confuse this parking area with the much larger parking area on the east side of I-70. There is no fee to park here. There are no restroom facilities.

**THE ROUTE:** Hike west past the gate up the asphalt road. After about 200 yards, go right and leave the road at a well-marked junction. Follow the rocky trail along North Tenmile Creek as it climbs steadily up the valley between Wichita Mountain (south) and Chief Mountain (north). Look for evidence of mining activity from the past along the way. At about 0.4 mile stay right at an unmarked fork in the trail. At 0.7 mile (9,544 feet) there is a small waterfall in the creek. At 2.0 miles (9,715 feet), enter the Eagles Nest Wilderness Area. At 2.5 miles (9,846 feet), cross a stream before entering an open meadow, which is a good place for wildflowers in the summer. At 3.1 miles (9,990 feet), reach a short side trail on your left leading down to a waterfall in the creek—definitely worth a look. At 3.4 miles (10,020 feet), arrive at the Gore Range Trail junction. To return to the trailhead and the parking area, reverse your route.

Waterfall in North Tenmile Creek.

## OPTIONS

**NORTH TENMILE CREEK TRAILHEAD TO MEADOW CREEK TRAILHEAD:** Total distance: 10.4 miles; 2,360 feet up.

Consider linking this hike with the Eccles Pass hike (Hike 12). From the intersection of the North Tenmile Creek Trail and the Gore Range Trail, go right and take the Gore Range Trail north, up out of the valley, and connect to the Meadow Creek Trail below Eccles Pass. From there, follow the Meadow Creek Trail back down to Frisco. This hike requires a car shuttle as you will not return to your starting point. If you decide to climb up to Eccles Pass too, add another 1.4 miles and 500 feet elevation gain to your trip.

**NORTH TENMILE CREEK TRAILHEAD (FRISCO) TO COPPER MOUNTAIN:** Total trip: 12.8 miles; 3,280 feet up, 2,760 feet down.

This hike is the reverse route of the hike described in the OPTIONS of the Uneva Pass hike (Hike 13). It starts in Frisco at the North Tenmile Creek Trailhead and finishes at Copper Mountain.

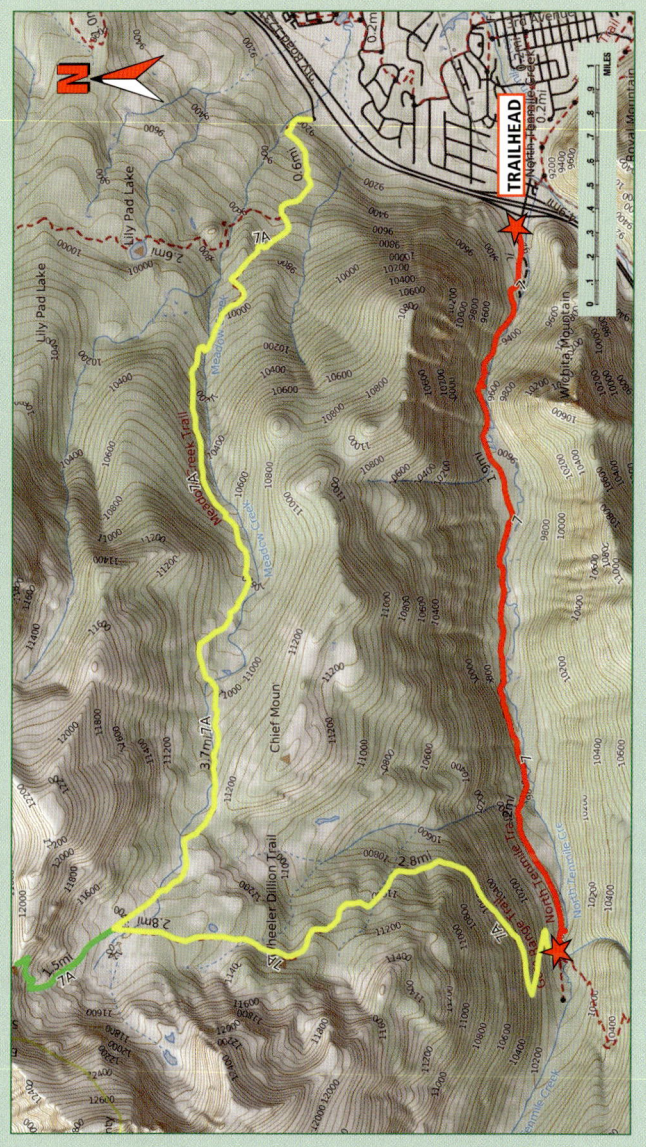

# 8. Continental Divide Overlook

| | |
|---|---|
| **RATING** | Moderate |
| **ROUND-TRIP DISTANCE** | 6.2 miles |
| **ROUND-TRIP TIME** | 5.0 hours |
| **ELEVATION GAIN** | 1,687 feet |
| **TRAILHEAD** | Interstate 70 west side of Eisenhower Tunnel, west-bound parking (11,145 feet) (13S 0419544E 4392503N) |
| **MAPS** | Trails Illustrated 104 Idaho Springs, Georgetown, Loveland Pass; USGS Loveland Pass Quadrangle |
| **NEAREST LANDMARK** | Eisenhower-Johnson Memorial Tunnel on I-70 |

**OVERVIEW:** This hike starts next to the Eisenhower Tunnel on Interstate 70 and takes you high up to the Continental Divide for spectacular views of Summit and Clear Creek counties. The first part of this hike climbs along the upper reaches of Straight Creek and the wildflowers that fill this area in the summer. As you approach the top, you are 1,500 feet directly above the tunnel. Almost entirely above treeline, the combination of great views and beautiful wildflowers make this hike special. Loveland, Keystone, and Breckenridge ski areas are all visible from the top. Pick a clear, sunny day to do this hike.

This trail is not recommended for winter use due to potential avalanche danger.

**GETTING THERE:** The parking area for this hike is along the westbound lanes of I-70, immediately on the west side of the Eisenhower-Johnson Memorial Tunnel. You must be traveling westbound through the tunnel in order to get to this parking area. If you are coming from Summit County

View of Keystone from the Continental Divide.

on I-70, go through the tunnel on the eastbound side, make a U-turn at the first exit on the east side of the tunnel (Loveland Pass exit 216), and drive back through the tunnel on the westbound side.

Stay in the slow lane as you approach the end of the tunnel. When you come out of the tunnel on the west side, you will immediately pull into the large parking area on your right. Park at the west end of the parking area, inside the white lines. Be sure to read and obey all signs. There is no fee to park. There are no public restroom facilities.

**THE ROUTE:** From the parking area, walk northeast up the paved road and pass the tunnel office building on the north side. Just beyond the building, the road turns right, then left, and begins to head northeast, away from the busy tunnel traffic. At 0.5 mile, the asphalt ends and the trail continues straight along a dirt road for about another 100 paces before leaving the road. Follow the trail up along the valley floor, just above Straight Creek, for another 0.75 mile. Summer wildflower viewing all along this section of the trail is exceptional.

At 1.2 miles (11,840 feet), the trail turns sharply and begins to climb up the side of the divide. After contouring

View of Grays & Torreys from the Continental Divide.

south and then hiking through a big switchback, you will arrive at the ridge and the trail will ease significantly. You are now on the Continental Divide. Continue south along the ridge and at 2.6 miles (12,500 feet) you will arrive at a point along the boundary markers of the Loveland Ski Area. Don't hike into the ski area. Instead, go right and follow the faint trail west and then south, again along the ridge to the obvious highpoint just west of the top of a chairlift (Chair 9) at Loveland Ski Area. At 3.1 miles (12,701 feet) you will reach the highpoint.

The views are panoramic. In addition to standing on the Continental Divide, you are also on the border between Summit and Clear Creek counties. To the southeast Torreys Peak (14,367 feet) and Grays Peak (14,270 feet) rise above the rest. Keystone Ski Resort is to the south with Mt. Guyot (13,370 feet) and Bald Mountain (13,684 feet) behind. To the right of these are Breckenridge and the Tenmile Range. In the distance on the southwest horizon is the Holy Cross Wilderness Area and Mount of the Holy Cross (14,005 feet). Due west, beyond the I-70 corridor, is the Gore Range.

To return to the parking area, reverse your route. You are 3.1 miles away.

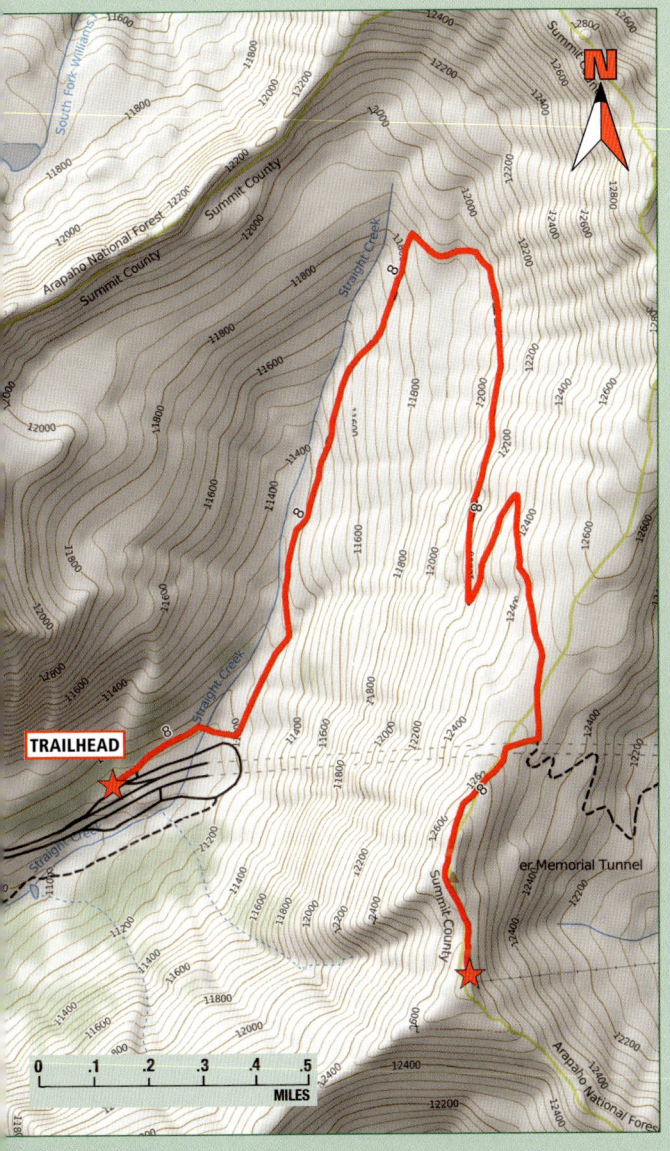

CONTINENTAL DIVIDE OVERLOOK 49

# 9. Peaks Trail

| | |
|---|---|
| **RATING** | Moderate |
| **ROUND-TRIP DISTANCE** | 7.9 miles |
| **ROUND-TRIP TIME** | 5.0 hours |
| **ELEVATION GAIN** | 763 feet |
| **TRAILHEAD** | Peaks Trail Trailhead Breckenridge (10,030 feet) (13S 0408219E 4371434N) |
| **MAPS** | Trails Illustrated 109 Breckenridge, Tennessee Pass; Trails Illustrated 108 Vail, Frisco, Dillon; USGS Frisco 7.5 minute |
| **NEAREST LANDMARK** | Breckenridge |
| **OPTIONS** | Ride the BreckConnect Gondola to the trailhead<br>Ride the Summit Stage bus back from Frisco |

**OVERVIEW:** This is a popular, moderate hike on rolling terrain over an easy trail through forest that takes you from Breckenridge to Frisco. The route, as described here, is mostly downhill and requires either a car shuttle or a bus ride from Frisco back to Breckenridge (more below).

You will encounter many creek and stream crossings during this hike, but all have well-built wooden bridges. There is no point along the trail where it is necessary to walk in water (but waterproof hiking boots are recommended). Mosquitoes can also be a problem in the wet areas.

Motorized vehicles are not allowed on this trail, but mountain bikes and horses are. Remember that bikes yield to hikers, and hikers yield to horses. This hike makes for an excellent snowshoe or Nordic ski day in the winter months.

**GETTING THERE:** Because the Peaks Trail is a point-to-point hike, it has two trailheads; one in Breckenridge and one in Frisco.

**BRECKENRIDGE TRAILHEAD:** From the traffic light intersection of Main Street and Ski Hill Road in the middle of Breckenridge, go west on Ski Hill Road up toward the ski resort. Go 1.9 miles from this intersection all the way to the top of Ski Hill Road, where you will pass the Peak 8 base area, and continue past the Peak 7 base area. The trailhead is on your

Trail sign along the Peaks Trail.

left, just past the Peak 7 base area. Parking is limited here (around 10 spots), so get there early. There is no fee to park here. There are no restroom facilities.

Another approach is to park down in Breckenridge and ride the gondola up to the trailhead (see Options).

**FRISCO TRAILHEAD:** From the corner of Main Street and 2nd Ave., head south on 2nd Ave. for about 0.5 mile. Take a right on Cabin Green, cross the recreation path (use caution here), and enter the trailhead parking area. Look for a bench with a Zach's Stop sign above it. This parking area is popular and fills on weekends. There is no fee to park here. There are no restroom facilities. See OPTIONS below for an alternative transportation strategy.

**THE ROUTE:** Find the obvious trailhead sign on the west side of the parking area. Head northwest up the well-worn trail as it enters tall conifer forest. The trail is marked sporadically

View of Tenmile Range from the Peaks Trail.

with plastic blue diamonds nailed to the trees. These marks are especially useful for winter travel. At 0.6 mile cross Cucumber Creek. Immediately after this crossing, cross a dirt road and continue on the trail on the other side. This road is the service road for the Breckenridge Ski Resort Peak 6 area. At 1.4 miles, cross South Barton Creek. At 2.8 miles, cross Middle Barton Creek. Note the sign on the west side of the bridge. Also note the water gate that controls flow into the small man-made canal that runs along the trail from this point for the next 0.4 mile. At 3.5 miles, cross North Barton Creek. Here two water gates control flow into two more man-made canals. The west canal follows the trail briefly.

At around 3.8 miles, the trail turns up into a small open meadow. This meadow is approximately the halfway point. To the east, Mt. Guyot (13,370 feet) (left) and Bald Mountain (13,684 feet) (right) dominate the skyline. Trees in this meadow were cut by the forest service to increase wildlife habitat and improve the health of the forest by creating age and species diversity. Wild roses are plentiful here in early July. A small log bench along the trail makes for a good place to take a break.

At 4.7 miles, you will reach the Miners Creek Trail junction. Follow the well-marked signs and continue straight on the Peaks Trail, which now briefly joins the Continental Divide Trail and the Colorado Trail. At 5.0 miles you will reach the Gold Hill Trail junction. Along this stretch of the trail, enjoy dramatic views of the Tenmile Range to the west. Continue straight on the Peaks Trail. At around 6.0 miles, you will cross Miners Creek two times, and at 6.9 miles pop out onto Miners Creek Road. Cross the road (and the creek) and follow the Rainbow Lake/Peaks Trailhead sign. At 7.1 miles, you will reach Rainbow Lake. Just past the lake, continue on the Peaks Trail past the Masontown Trail junction sign. Shortly after this point, at about 7.75 miles, be careful to go left at an unmarked fork in the trail. At 7.9 miles, pass the Bill's Ranch Trail junction sign.

At 7.9 miles, near the end of the trail, you will reach a Peaks Trail sign indicating distances: Rainbow Lake 1, Gold Hill Trail 3, Breckenridge 8. Head due west for another 100 yards to reach the Frisco Trailhead parking area.

## OPTIONS

**BRECKENRIDGE GONDOLA RIDE TO PEAK 7:** An alternative to driving to the trailhead is to park down in Breckenridge, ride the BreckConnect gondola up to Peak 7, and walk over to the trailhead. Both the parking and the gondola ride are free. Park in the huge lot at the corner of North French St. and Highway 9. Restroom facilities are available. Get off the gondola at the second stop (Peak 7 station—about 9 minutes) and make your way down to Ski Hill Road. Head north

Easy trail through the woods.

for about 0.25 mile along the road, past the Peak 7 base area to the trailhead on your left. You can combine this option with the next one to end the day back at your car.

**COUNTY COMMONS LIBRARY BUS STOP:** Instead of dropping a car in Frisco or coordinating a pick up, consider taking the Summit Stage bus back to Breckenridge. When you arrive at Miners Creek Road, instead of continuing on the Peaks Trail, go right onto Miners Creek Road and follow it out to the recreation path and down to the County Commons buildings (about 1.0 mile total). The County Commons bus stop is on the north side of the library. The bus to Breckenridge stops there every 30 minutes throughout the summer months. The bus will take you to the gondola parking lot without any transfers required. The bus is free. For more information call the Summit Stage, (970) 296-8111.

PEAKS TRAIL

# 10. Mohawk Lakes

| | |
|---|---|
| **RATING** | Moderate |
| **ROUND-TRIP DISTANCE** | 6.6 miles |
| **ROUND-TRIP TIME** | 5.0 hours |
| **ELEVATION GAIN** | 1,750 feet |
| **TRAILHEAD** | Spruce Creek Trailhead (10,400 feet) (13S 0409592E 4365799N) |
| **MAPS** | Trails Illustrated 109 Breckenridge, Tennessee Pass; USGS Breckenridge Quadrangle |
| **NEAREST LANDMARK** | Breckenridge |
| **OPTIONS** | Mayflower Lake (11,300 feet) Upper Mohawk Lake Trail (12,450 feet) |

**OVERVIEW:** Just south of Breckenridge, this hike starts at 10,400 feet and climbs up to Mohawk Lake at 12,090 feet. The trail follows Spruce Creek west through dense forest before climbing up to the base of Continental Falls, a 400-foot waterfall cascading down from Lower Mohawk Lake. Pass the well-preserved remains of an old mining site along the way. Above Lower Mohawk Lake, the trail heads up to Mohawk Lake, a beautiful alpine lake in a picturesque setting. For a longer day, tack on the more strenuous Upper Mohawk Lakes Trail. Much less traveled, the Upper Mohawk Lakes Trail continues higher to a series of alpine lakes at the top of the valley. Views of the valley headwall and surrounding mountains are fantastic (see OPTIONS).

**GETTING THERE:** From the intersection of Highway 9 and Boreas Pass Road on the south side of Breckenridge, head south on Highway 9 for about 2.1 miles. Watch for the

Lower Mohawk Lake.

street sign for Spruce Creek Road (CR 800) on your right (west side of highway). Take a sharp right onto Spruce Creek Road, follow it up a short hill, and then bear left at the first intersection. Continue on Spruce Creek Road for approximately 1.1 miles where you will reach the trailhead parking area. This parking area is moderately large (it holds about 60 vehicles) but fills up quickly on weekends. There is no fee to park here. There are no restroom facilities.

Note that it is possible to drive past the trailhead up Spruce Creek Road for another 1.8 miles to the McCullough Tunnel area. The road to this area requires a four-wheel-drive vehicle, is accessible in summer only, and there are only a few parking spaces; it is not recommended.

**THE ROUTE:** Find the obvious trailhead sign on the south side of the parking area. Don't hike up the road. The sign indicates it is 3.4 miles to Mohawk Lakes. Follow the obvious trail in a southwesterly direction. At about 0.1 mile, the

Mohawk Lake.

trail has a fork where an unmarked social trail goes to the left. Stay right and keep Spruce Creek on your left. Note the occasional blue diamonds nailed to the trees along the trail. These marks are especially useful for winter travel. At just under 0.5 mile, the trail crosses Spruce Creek and continues southwest along the other side of the creek. At 1.5 miles, you will reach the well-marked Wheeler Trail junction. Continue straight on the Spruce Creek Trail and pass by a small open meadow on your right. At 1.7 miles, the trail crosses the creek again.

At just under 2.0 miles, the trail pops out on Spruce Creek Road near the McCullough water diversion tunnel. Follow the road up to the left for about 200 feet to the diversion gates. Pick up the trail on your right as it leaves the road and enters the forest again. At 2.2 miles you will reach the well-marked Mayflower Lake Trail junction. Go left and continue up toward the Mohawk Lakes. You will pass the remains of a log cabin on your right and then cross the creek. Follow the trail carefully from here as it steepens and begins to climb a large granite outcrop wall. At 2.5 miles, you will reach the remains of two log cabins. The lower portion of Continental Falls is on your right. Note that the main trail goes left here (as indicated by the sign) but a "lower falls vista" is to the right. This vista is worth the time and is a good place to take a break. Take great care on the rocks near the falls.

Continue up the trail as it switchbacks up to the left (south) of the falls. Farther up you will pass the remains of a cable wheel once used for mining. Follow the trail as it continues up behind this area. At just under 3.0 miles, you will reach Lower Mohawk Lake. For a shorter hike, make this your turn-around spot. To continue up, follow the trail around the south side of the lake and then up another steep rock wall. Follow the trail carefully through this section as it is sometimes ambiguous. At 3.5 miles, you will arrive at eye-level with Mohawk Lake. On windy days, it is significantly colder at this lake than it is at the lower lake, even in the summer. Fishing at these lakes is popular. For most, this is the turn-around point of the hike.

To return to the trailhead and the parking area, reverse your route. Take into consideration that, even though it's mostly downhill, you are 3.3 miles away.

## OPTIONS

**MAYFLOWER LAKE:** Additional round-trip: 0.2 miles; 20 feet up.

This is a very easy extension to this hike. Take the short spur up to Mayflower Lake from the Mayflower Lake junction. This small lake at the base of the south side of Mt. Helen makes a good place to take a break. Fishing is popular here.

Alpine Lake on Upper Mohawk Lake Trail.

**UPPER MOHAWK LAKE TRAIL:** Additional round-trip: 2.6 miles; 385 feet up.

For the more adventurous, continue past Mohawk Lake and climb the rock wall up to Upper Mohawk Lake Trail. Entirely above treeline, this trail heads west across alpine meadows to a series of unnamed lakes offering dramatic views in all directions. Pacific Peak (13,950 feet) sits at the south end of the glacial cirque at the valley headwall. In the summer months, wildflowers flourish along the creeks joining these lakes. This hike is well worth the extra effort, but note that the trail is less traveled and not as easy to follow. The trail between the third and fourth lakes is non-existent but the direction is clear. Get an early start if you plan to do this one. To return to the parking area, reverse your route.

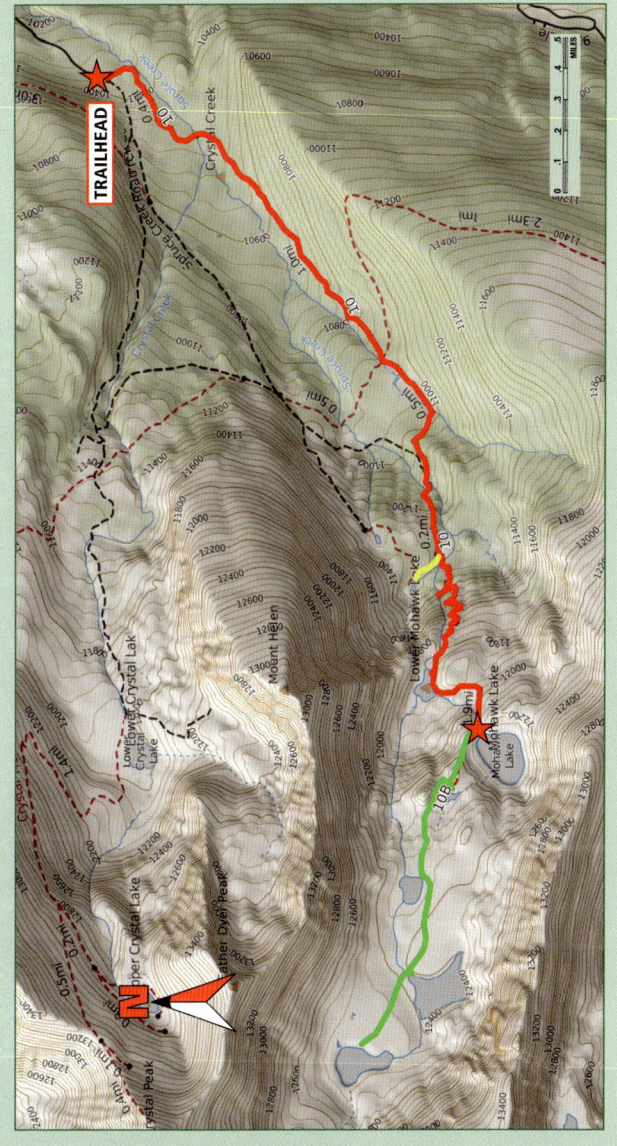

MOHAWK LAKES 61

# 11. Argentine Pass

| | |
|---|---|
| **RATING** | Moderate |
| **ROUND-TRIP DISTANCE** | 5.2 miles |
| **ROUND-TRIP TIME** | 5.0 hours |
| **ELEVATION GAIN** | 2,168 feet |
| **TRAILHEAD** | Argentine Pass Trailhead (11,300 feet) (13S 0431634E 4385172N) |
| **MAPS** | Trails Illustrated 104 Idaho Springs, Georgetown, Loveland Pass; USGS Montezuma, USGS Grays Peak Quadrangles |
| **NEAREST LANDMARK** | Montezuma |

**OVERVIEW:** This hike starts at Peru Creek in Horseshoe Basin and climbs up to Argentine Pass on the Continental Divide. The trail follows what is left of the historic Argentine Pass wagon road, once the primary route between Clear Creek and Summit counties. This high-altitude trek starts at over 11,000 feet and climbs 2,100 feet in just over 2.5 miles. Views from the pass are spectacular, both to the east and the west. Rich in mining history, the first major discovery of silver ore in Colorado was made in this basin and evidence of those mining days still remains. The mountain and pass were named Argentine from the Latin word for silver, *argentum*.

**GETTING THERE:** Travel east from Dillon on Highway 6 toward Keystone. Just past the Keystone Ski Resort exit, turn right onto Montezuma Road. Don't go up toward Loveland Pass. Follow Montezuma Road for 4.3 miles to Peru Creek Road 260. Turn left and follow unpaved Peru Creek Road north and then west for 4.4 miles to a parking area on your left. This is the parking area for the Argentine Pass Trail. Don't go past the parking area. The road is gated just around the

Hiking along the Argentine Pass trail.

bend and there is no place to park. Do not block the gate. Note that Peru Creek Road is a little rough and rocky but does not require a four-wheel-drive vehicle. Allow 20 minutes to drive it each way. There is no fee to park here. There are no restroom facilities.

**THE ROUTE:** From the parking area hike northeast up the road, past the retired ore loading station, to the gate. Continue past the gate and at 0.4 mile (11,300 feet) look for the Argentine Pass Trail on your right. Leave the road and follow the trail southeast. Cross Peru Creek on a sturdy wooden bridge and continue through a dense willow patch south, up through a wooded area to treeline.

From here the trail up to the pass is one giant switchback followed by a long contouring traverse. Because this route was originally used as a wagon road, the average incline was kept to a minimum. The trail is mostly over rock talus but stays relatively even and easy to follow, even without the help of cairns. Start by climbing the increasingly rocky trail southeast, up to around 11,850 feet, where it makes a 180-degree turn to the north. Follow the trail as it climbs steadily along the broad west face of Argentine Peak. Imagine riding up this in a mule-drawn wagon in the late 1800s! The valley headwall and Grays Peak (14,270

Old mining loader near the parking area.

feet), immediately to the northwest, tower over Horseshoe Basin. At about 12,600 feet, climb a small step that requires handholds. Continue up the long catwalk and at 2.6 miles (13,207 feet) reach Argentine Pass.

Views from the pass are spectacular. Directly south along the Continental Divide is Argentine Peak (13,738 feet). To the northwest over the right shoulder of Grays Peak is Torreys Peak (14,267 feet). To the east, the tops of Mt. Bierstadt (14,060 feet) and Mt. Evans (14,264 feet) stand high above the neighboring mountains. To the southwest, the Tenmile Range and Quandary Peak (14,265 feet) are visible on the horizon.

While motorized vehicle travel is prohibited on the west side of the pass, it is allowed on the east side. You may encounter jeeps or other vehicles coming up from the other side, along the old wagon trail. Argentine Pass is one of the highest named vehicle-accessible passes in the state. It is also the boundary between Summit and Clear Creek counties. Enjoy the history and the views. To return to the trailhead and the parking area, reverse your route.

Because Peru Creek Road is not snowplowed, winter access to this trail requires a very long approach. Avalanche danger is also a threat during the winter months.

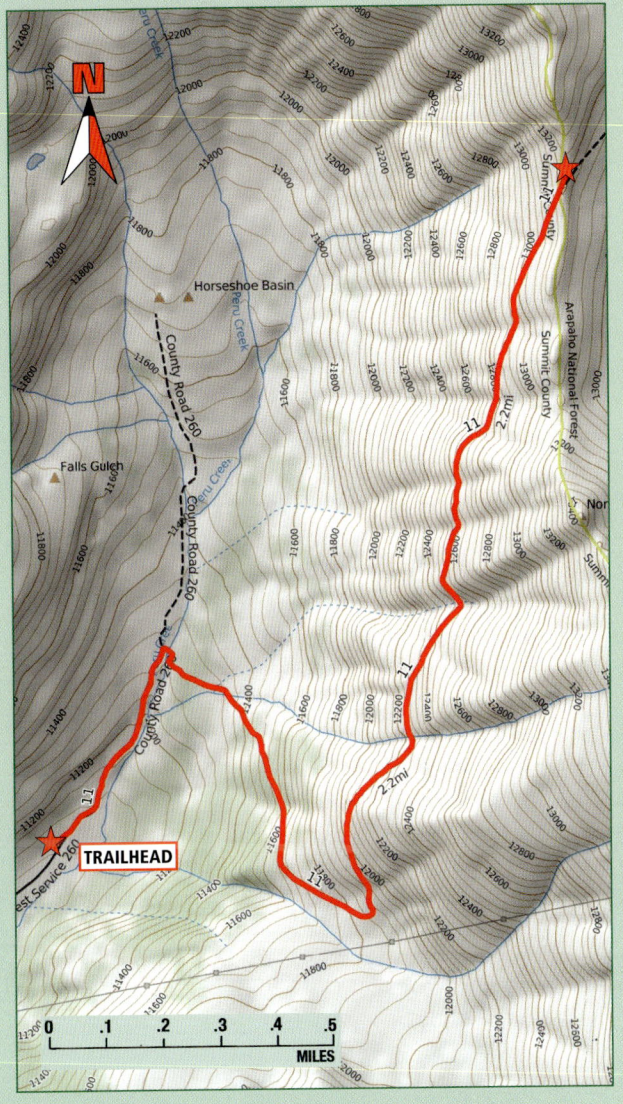

# 12. Eccles Pass

| | |
|---|---|
| **RATING** | Moderate-Difficult |
| **ROUND-TRIP DISTANCE** | 10.0 miles |
| **ROUND-TRIP TIME** | 6.0 hours |
| **ELEVATION GAIN** | 2,750 feet |
| **TRAILHEAD** | Meadow Creek Trailhead (9,160 feet) (13S 0405030E 4382728N) |
| **MAPS** | Trails Illustrated 108 Vail, Frisco, Dillon; USGS Dillon, USGS Vail Pass Quadrangles |
| **NEAREST LANDMARK** | Frisco |
| **OPTIONS** | Eccles Peak (12,313 feet) Deming Mountain (12,902 feet) |

**OVERVIEW:** This is a great moderate–difficult hike close to Frisco with fantastic views of the southern Gore Range, Dillon Reservoir, and Copper Mountain Ski Area. The trail is well maintained and easy to follow. The hike reaches Eccles Pass along the Gore Range Trail. This hike is very popular year-round and makes an excellent snowshoe route in the winter.

**GETTING THERE:** The trailhead is on the north side of Interstate 70, just west of the exit 203 roundabout. You must use the roundabout on the north side of I-70 to access this trailhead. Once in the roundabout, take the exit clearly marked with the Meadow Creek Trailhead sign. Follow this unpaved, graded road about 0.5 mile to the trailhead parking area. The parking area is exceptionally large but can fill up on weekends in the summer. Go early. There is no fee to park here. There are no restroom facilities.

**THE ROUTE:** In the parking area, find the obvious Meadow Creek Trail sign in the northeast corner of the lot. Follow the trail north and then west as it climbs first through tall

Eccles Pass from the Meadow Creek Trail.

aspen and then lodgepole forests. At 0.5 mile, you will pass the remains of an old log cabin on your left and then at 0.6 mile, reach the clearly marked trail junction to Lily Pad Lakes. Continue straight on the Meadow Creek Trail and enter the Eagles Nest Wilderness Area. At 1.4 miles you will cross Meadow Creek on a solid flat-log bridge. This is the first of three crossings over this creek. Continue up the trail as it follows the Meadow Creek drainage basin. At 3.0 miles you will cross the creek again on a makeshift log bridge. Don't follow the weak trail to your left; cross the creek and pick up the trail on the other side. At 4.0 miles, you will cross Meadow Creek for the third time.

The trail now enters the top of the Meadow Creek drainage basin and the valley opens into a broad meadow with views in all directions. The low point on the ridge to the north is your destination: Eccles Pass. Deming Mountain (12,902 feet) is immediately to the west. At mile 4.2, you will reach the Gore Range Trail junction. Go straight onto the Gore Range Trail and continue northwest up toward the pass. This area offers the quintessential Colorado alpine wildflower viewing experience in July and August. If possible, go then, but don't forget to bring the bug spray. Just below the pass, the trail steepens and then climbs switchbacks up to Eccles Pass at mile 5.0 (11,900 feet).

Views from Eccles Pass include Buffalo Mountain (12,777 feet) to the northeast, Red Peak (13,189 feet) and Mt. Silverthorne (13,357 feet) (behind Red Peak to the left) to the north, and Deming Mountain (12,902 feet) to the west. You can see that the Gore Range Trail continues down the other side of Eccles Pass into the South Willow Creek Basin. The low point in the north-south ridge on your left, just over a mile away, is Red Buffalo Pass (Hike 14).

To return to the trailhead and the parking area, reverse your route. Take into consideration that, even though it's mostly downhill, you are 5.0 miles away from the parking area.

## OPTIONS

**ECCLES PEAK:** Additional round trip: 1.2 miles; 400 feet up.

Head east from Eccles Pass up the ridgeline for another 0.6 miles and 410 feet (one-way) to the summit of Eccles Peak. The views from Eccles Peak are worth the extra effort for those so inclined but this extension does add over an hour to the overall hike time. Do not do this extension if the weather is doubtful as it is all above treeline and exposed to lightning.

**DEMING MOUNTAIN:** Additional round-trip: 1.4 miles; 1,150 feet up.

For the more adventurous, this hike up to the summit of Deming Mountain rewards the effort. Note that this is an off-trail hike and requires some (very easy) route finding to the top. Leave the Gore Range Trail near the start of the switchbacks that climb up to Eccles Pass (it is possible to go directly from the top of Eccles Pass, but this requires crossing much more rock). Head straight for the shallow rock band that is directly in front of you and pick one of the many grassy slopes up through this area. Continue to navigate around rock patches as you climb toward the obvious summit. Find the BLM survey marker at the high point of the summit and enjoy the views. The heart of the southern Gore Range is directly to the north, and the peak immediately to the west is West Deming (12,736 feet).

ECCLES PASS

# 13. Uneva Pass

| | |
|---|---|
| **RATING** | Moderate-Difficult |
| **ROUND-TRIP DISTANCE** | 12.4 miles |
| **ROUND-TRIP TIME** | 8.0 hours |
| **ELEVATION GAIN** | 2,580 feet |
| **TRAILHEAD** | Wheeler/Gore Range Trailhead (9,665 feet) (13S 0401419E 4374876N) |
| **MAPS** | Trails Illustrated 108 Vail, Frisco, Dillon; USGS Vail Pass Quadrangle |
| **NEAREST LANDMARK** | Copper Mountain |
| **OPTIONS** | Wheeler Lakes (11,070 feet) Copper Mountain to North Ten Mile Trailhead in Frisco |

**OVERVIEW:** More of a moderate–difficult hike due to the distance, this hike starts near Copper Mountain and takes you up to Uneva Pass in the Eagles Nest Wilderness Area. Starting at 9,665 feet, right along Interstate 70, the trail climbs up through aspen and conifer forest past the Wheeler Lakes Trail junction at 11,060 feet (see OPTIONS) and Lost Lake at 11,600 feet before finally climbing up to Uneva Pass at 11,926 feet. Enjoy panoramic views of Uneva Peak and the Gore Range from the pass.

For a longer day, consider connecting this hike to the North Tenmile Creek trail (Hike 7) (see OPTIONS).

**GETTING THERE:** Access is a little tricky; you must be heading west on I-70 toward Copper Mountain to get to the parking area for this trailhead. Take the Scenic Area exit just before the Copper Mountain exit. If you reach the Copper Mountain exit (exit 195), you've gone too far. If you're heading east on I-70 from Copper Mountain, U-turn at Officer's Gulch (exit 198) and get back on I-70 heading west. Park at

Uneva Pass from Wheeler Lakes.

the south end of the parking area, near the trailhead. There is no fee to park. There are no restroom facilities.

**THE ROUTE:** Find the trailhead kiosk at the south end of the parking area and follow the Gore Range Trail sign across a small bridge to a dirt road. Turn left and hike the dirt road south along I-70. At 0.8 mile, the road narrows to a path and passes another trail sign and kiosk. Follow the trail to the right as it finally begins to climb up away from I-70 and at 1.6 miles (10,184 feet) pass the Eagles Nest Wilderness Boundary sign. Now in dense forest, continue up for another 0.75 mile where the slope eases somewhat near an open meadow. At 3.0 miles (11,060 feet) reach the Wheeler Lakes Trail junction. For a shorter day, take this short spur trail over to the Wheeler Lakes (see OPTIONS).

Past Wheeler Lakes, the trail heads northwest through alternating forest, meadows, and wetlands. This area is great for wildflower viewing in the summer. At 4.5 miles (11,380 feet), cross a long wooden bridge over a wetlands area. This bridge was built without the use of power tools (which are not allowed in the wilderness area, even for trail maintenance). At 5.3 miles (11,600 feet) arrive at Lost Lake, a good place to take a break. From here the trail steepens as it climbs out of the trees up to the pass, now visible ahead. At 6.2 miles (11,926 feet) reach the top of Uneva Pass.

The views from the pass are outstanding. To the south is Copper Mountain Ski Area and Jacque Peak (13,205 feet).

Beyond Copper Mountain is the Tenmile Range. Immediately to the northwest are Uneva Peak (12,522 feet) and the beautiful drainage basin below it that feeds into North Tenmile Creek. To the north is the Gore Range.

To return to the trailhead, reverse your route. Take into consideration that, even though it's mostly downhill, you are 6.2 miles away.

## OPTIONS

**WHEELER LAKES:** Total round-trip from the trailhead: 6.8 miles; 1,460 feet up.

Take the short Wheeler Lakes Spur Trail from the Gore Range Trail to visit these two beautiful alpine lakes. Wildflowers thrive in the wetlands near the lakes. Uneva Pass is visible to the northwest. Wheeler Lakes makes a great destination for a shorter day. It also makes a good snowshoe route in the winter.

**COPPER MOUNTAIN TO NORTH TENMILE CREEK TRAILHEAD (FRISCO):** Total trip: 12.8 miles; 2,760 feet up; 3,280 feet down.

Continue north from Uneva Pass down the Gore Range Trail for 3.4 miles to the North Tenmile Creek Trail junction. From there, follow the North Tenmile Creek Trail east for 3.4 miles, back out to Frisco (Hike 7). The route crosses the open drainage basin southeast of Uneva Peak, reenters the forest, and then drops 1,500 feet down into the North Tenmile Creek valley. Cross the creek and find the North Tenmile Creek Trail immediately on the other side. Go right and leave the Gore Range Trail. Hike east on this easy trail to the North Tenmile Creek Trailhead in Frisco (I-70 exit 201). This hike requires a car shuttle as you will not be returning to where you started. This hike can be done in either direction but the route from Copper to Frisco (described here) is 520 feet less in elevation gain.

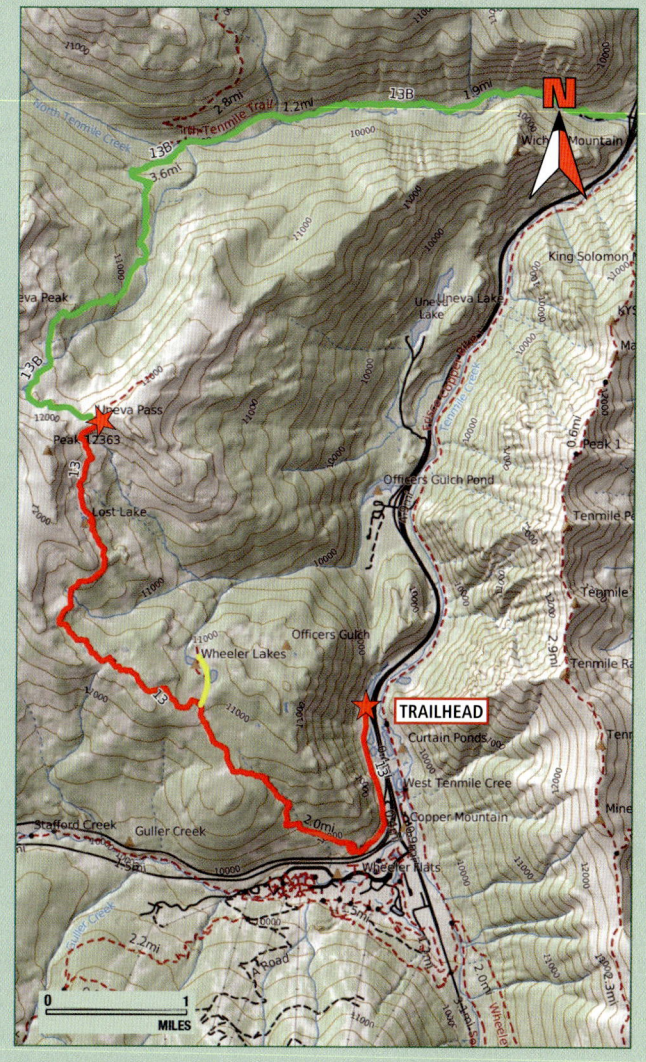

# 14. Red Buffalo Pass

| | |
|---|---|
| **RATING** | Moderate-Difficult |
| **ROUND-TRIP DISTANCE** | 12.4 miles |
| **ROUND-TRIP TIME** | 8.0 hours |
| **ELEVATION GAIN** | 2,835 feet |
| **TRAILHEAD** | Willowbrook Trailhead (8,986 feet) (13S 0405792E 4389661N) |
| **MAPS** | Trails Illustrated 108 Vail, Frisco, Dillon; USGS Frisco, USGS Dillon, USGS Willow Lakes, USGS Vail Pass Quadrangles |
| **NEAREST LANDMARK** | Silverthorne |
| **OPTIONS** | Red Peak<br>Buffalo Mountain Loop<br>Gore Creek Trail to East Vail |

**OVERVIEW:** This hike starts in Silverthorne and takes you up to Red Buffalo Pass in the Eagles Nest Wilderness Area. Starting at 9,000 feet, the trail climbs gradually through the narrow valley between Buffalo Mountain and Red Peak. Stop at South Willow Falls along the way, or make that your destination for the day. Continue higher along South Willow Creek Basin to treeline and then up to Red Buffalo Pass at 11,755 feet. From the pass, enjoy excellent views in all directions. Look west down into Gore Creek Valley, all the way to Vail. Do this hike in late July or early August for an unbelievable wildflower show.

This hike has some challenging options (see OPTIONS). Winter use above the falls is not recommended due to avalanche danger.

**GETTING THERE:** Head north on Highway 9 in Silverthorne from the Interstate 70 exit (exit 205) for approximately 2.0 miles and turn left on Willowbrook Road. Follow Willowbrook

Red Buffalo Pass and Red Peak above South Willow Creek Basin. View from Eccles Pass.

Road west for 1.0 mile to the trailhead parking area. This trailhead is in a residential neighborhood and is small, with about 13 parking spaces. Get there early. Overnight parking is not allowed. There are no restroom facilities. There is no parking fee.

**THE ROUTE:** Find the trailhead at the west end of the parking area and follow the trail for about 50 paces to a trail junction. Turn left and follow the South Willowbrook Trail sign. Continue along this well-traveled trail west into the forest and immediately cross North Willow Creek and Middle Willow Creek on some flat-log bridges. At 0.3 mile (9,154 feet) pass the Eagles Nest Wilderness Area boundary sign. At 1.1 miles (9,419 feet) reach the Mesa Cortina Trail junction sign. Go right and head west on the Mesa Cortina Trail. At 1.5 miles (9,432 feet) reach the Gore Range Trail junction sign. Continue straight (west) on the Gore Range Trail. The trail is easy through here as it crosses forest and meadows with good views of Buffalo Mountain ahead. At 2.5 miles (9,642 feet) stay on the Gore Range Trail as you pass the South Willow/Buffalo Cabin Connect Trail sign on

Red Peak from South Willow Creek Basin.

your left. The trail gradually climbs up into the valley along South Willow Creek. At 3.1 miles (10,020 feet) reach the short spur trail over to South Willow Falls. Slab rocks along the falls make a great place to take a break. For a shorter day, the falls makes a good destination (6.2 miles round trip and 1,080 feet up from the trailhead). Use caution on slippery rocks along the falls.

Back on the Gore Range Trail at the South Willow Falls Trail junction, look carefully for the trail as it climbs sharply up to the right over the rocks. Don't go straight into a dead end campsite. After a few short switchbacks up the rocks, the trail heads west again up the valley between Buffalo Mountain and Red Peak. This long straightaway crosses several small streams flowing down from Red Peak.

As you near treeline, the trail turns left and heads southwest before leaving the trees at 5.5 miles (11,388 feet). Identify Red Buffalo Pass. It's the low point on the north end of the headwall ridge. Follow the trail up to an unnamed lake. Take a sharp right at an unmarked trail junction and follow its left branch diagonally up the last 300 feet to the pass. At 6.2 miles (11,755 feet) reach the summit of Red Buffalo Pass.

Red Buffalo Pass is the border between Summit and Eagle counties. The headwaters of the Gore Creek flow down the valley on the west side of the pass into the Eagle River and eventually to the Colorado River. South Willow Creek Basin and the west face of Buffalo Mountain are to the east. The Gore Range Trail continues over Eccles Pass along the ridge to the south (Hike 12).

To return to the trailhead and the parking area, reverse your route. Take into consideration that, even though it's mostly downhill, you are 6.2 miles away.

## OPTIONS

**RED PEAK:** Additional round-trip: 2.4 miles; 1,477 feet up.

For the more adventurous, this additional scramble up to the summit of Red Peak (13,189 feet) is well worth the challenge. Note that this route is OFF-TRAIL and requires some easy route finding and rock scrambling. Follow the obvious ridgeline all the way to the summit, leaving it only briefly at one or two spots. The summit is visible from the pass. The 360-degree views from the top are well worth the effort. Do not attempt this climb if the weather is doubtful as it is all above treeline and exposed to lightning.

Eccles Pass from Red Buffalo Pass. Photo taken on July 4th..

Taking a break and enjoying the view near Red Buffalo Pass.

**BUFFALO MOUNTAIN LOOP:** Total trip: 12.5 miles; 3,200 feet up; 3,300 feet down.

Consider combining this hike with the Eccles Pass hike (Hike 12). It does not add much distance but it does require a car shuttle from the Meadow Creek Trailhead as you will not return to your starting point. Follow the trail back down the east side of Red Buffalo Pass toward the lake and stay on the Gore Range Trail as it heads south up to Eccles Pass. Hike down the south side of Eccles Pass and follow the trail out to the Meadow Creek Trailhead in Frisco. South Willow Creek Basin, due west of Buffalo Mountain, makes a great place to camp. There are no designated campsites, so follow all national forest and wilderness area camping-at-large rules.

**GORE CREEK TRAIL TO EAST VAIL (FROM RED BUFFALO PASS):** Total trip: 12.9 miles; 3,050 feet up; 3,350 feet down.

This hike takes you down the west side of Red Buffalo Pass into Eagle County. Follow the trail for 6.7 miles as it drops down into the Gore Creek Valley and continues all the way to East Vail. The trail is well defined and easy to follow but does require a significant creek crossing. This entire hike (from Silverthorne) can be done in one very long day but an overnight backpack is recommended. The natural beauty of this valley is worth the time. Also consider adding a night at Gore Lake. Transportation back from the East Vail trailhead is required. For more information, see the Trails Illustrated 108 Vail, Frisco, Dillon map. Additional research and planning is recommended.

# 15. Willow Lakes

| | |
|---|---|
| **RATING** | Moderate-Difficult |
| **ROUND-TRIP DISTANCE** | 11.8 miles |
| **ROUND-TRIP TIME** | 9.0 hours |
| **ELEVATION GAIN** | 2,728 feet |
| **TRAILHEAD** | Willowbrook Trailhead (8,986 feet) (13S 0405792E 4389661N) |
| **MAPS** | Trails Illustrated 108 Vail, Frisco, Dillon; USGS Willow Lakes, USGS Dillon Quadrangles |
| **NEAREST LANDMARK** | Silverthorne |
| **OPTIONS** | Salmon Lake (11,190 feet) |

**OVERVIEW:** This hike makes for a long day but is worth the effort. Almost entirely in the Eagles Nest Wilderness, this hike takes you through quiet forests to a spectacular alpine lake setting surrounded by jagged rocky peaks. The trail is long but well marked and easy to follow. Pick a day when the weather is good and start early. The cover picture of this book was taken along this trail.

**GETTING THERE:** Head north on Highway 9 in Silverthorne from the Interstate 70 exit (exit 205) for approximately 2.0 miles and turn left onto Willowbrook Road. Follow Willowbrook Road west for 1.0 mile to the trailhead parking area. This trailhead is in a residential neighborhood and is small, with about 13 parking spaces. Get there early. Overnight parking is not allowed. There are no restroom facilities. There is no parking fee.

**THE ROUTE:** Find the clearly marked start of the trail next to the parking area. Be careful with your route finding at the beginning of this trail. Go about 50 paces along the trail

North face of Red Peak.

to a well-marked trail junction. Take the Ditches Trail north (not the South Willowbrook Trail). Cross over some wooden bridges and follow the trail up behind a residential area before entering the forest. At 0.5 mile (9,260 feet) you will reach the clearly marked North Willow Creek Trail junction. Turn left here and head due west on the North Willow Creek Trail. Note that most maps of this trail route are incomplete or not accurate. At 1.0 mile (9,500 feet), pass the Three Peaks Trail junction and continue west on the North Willow Creek Trail. You will soon pass the Eagles Nest Wilderness Area boundary sign and come alongside the North Willow Creek. At 1.3 miles (9,580 feet) you will reach the clearly marked Gore Range Trail junction. Go straight onto the Gore Range Trail. Continue northwest on the Gore Range Trail for 1.5 miles and at mile 2.8 (10,330 feet), reach the clearly marked Willow Lakes Trail junction. Note that most maps show this trail junction in the wrong place. Leave the Gore Range Trail and follow the Willow Lakes Trail west and up. The trail steepens significantly over the next mile but levels off again at just over 11,000 feet and begins to contour high along the North Willow Creek drainage valley. Views across the valley of the north face of Red Peak come into view. At 4.4 miles (11,110 feet), reach the clearly marked Salmon Lake Trail junction. Continue left on the Willow Lakes Trail. The trail now enters the

View from Willow Lakes.

wetlands at the top of the Willow Lakes drainage. You will cross a creek and a series of small pools on makeshift log bridges—nothing too difficult. After this, the trail continues along the south side of a small lake and then up into a small meadow where the views begin to open up. The rugged north face of Red Peak (13,136 feet) looms large immediately to the south. Continue along the somewhat weaker trail as it heads back into the trees between the lakes. Stay the course; the best is yet to come! Follow the trail through the trees and at 5.9 miles (11,400 feet) you will finally reach the last lake. The jagged ridge that makes up the glacial cirque directly to the west is known unofficially as the Zodiac Spires; each pinnacle is named after one of the signs of the zodiac. Capricorn is the large block on the left. On the other side of the spires is Eagle County. The west end of Red Peak's massive north side is on your left (south), East Thorne Peak (13,333 feet) is on your right (north). Take a well-deserved break and enjoy the magnificent views.

To return to the trailhead and the parking area, reverse your route. Take into consideration that, even though it's mostly downhill, you are still almost 6 miles from the trailhead.

## OPTIONS

**SALMON LAKE:** Additional round-trip: 1.2 miles; 200 feet up.

This isolated lake sits north of the Willow Lakes at the base of East Thorne Peak (13,333 feet). Take the Salmon Lake Trail spur from the North Willow Creek Trail. Follow it west for 0.6 miles up to the far end of Salmon Lake at 11,200 feet. Salmon Lake makes a good camping and fishing destination. This is a more secluded destination. Be sure to take bug spray.

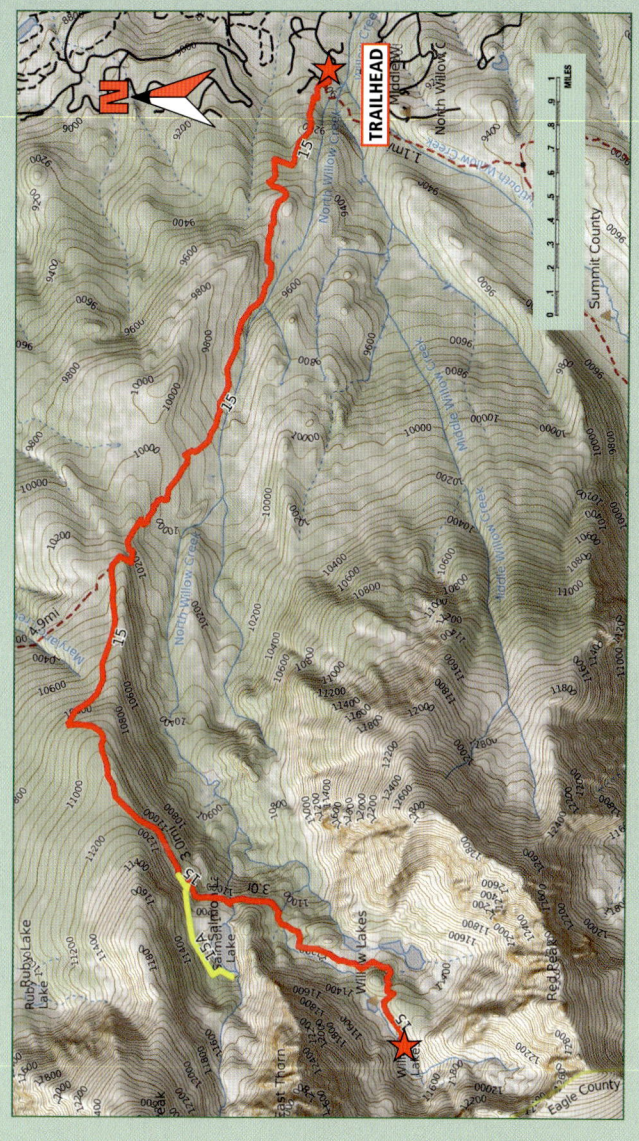

WILLOW LAKES

# 16. Ptarmigan Peak

| | |
|---|---|
| RATING | Difficult |
| ROUND-TRIP DISTANCE | 11.6 miles |
| ROUND-TRIP TIME | 7.0 hours |
| ELEVATION GAIN | 3,610 feet |
| TRAILHEAD | Ptarmigan Peak Trailhead (9,085 feet) (13S 0409599E 4387800N) |
| MAPS | Trails Illustrated 108 Vail, Frisco, Dillon; USGS Dillon Quadrangle |
| NEAREST LANDMARK | Silverthorne |

**OVERVIEW:** This hike takes you high into the Williams Fork Mountains to the Ptarmigan Peak Wilderness Area. At just over 12,000 acres, Ptarmigan is the smaller, less traveled of the two wilderness areas in Summit County. Starting in Silverthorne at just over 9,000 feet, the trail climbs gradually through mixed forest to treeline at about 11,500 feet. Above treeline the trail breaks out and crosses wide-open alpine meadows with spectacular views—some of the best in Summit County. The trail ends at 12,498 feet on the summit of Ptarmigan Peak. If you're lucky, you might see a ptarmigan along the way.

This hike is long and much of it is above treeline. Be sure to plan ahead, check the weather forecast, and get an early start.

This hike is also a popular snowshoe route during the winter months but following the trail is more difficult.

**GETTING THERE:** In Silverthorne, get in the right lane of Highway 9 heading north from Interstate 70 exit 205. Take a quick right onto Rainbow Drive (the first stoplight) and then another quick right onto Tanglewood Lane (the first stop sign). Follow Tanglewood Lane around a bend for 0.25

Dillon Reservoir from Ptarmigan Peak Wilderness.

mile to the stop sign. Go right at the stop sign onto Ptarmigan Trail and follow it east for 0.25 mile, where it changes into a dirt road at a curve (go straight). Continue east on the dirt road for another 0.50 mile. The trailhead parking area is on your right. There is no fee to park here. There are no restroom facilities.

**THE ROUTE:** Find the trailhead kiosk at the east end of the parking area. Head north up the trail through a residential area and after about 0.1 mile, pop out on an asphalt road. Follow the road straight up the hill for another 150 paces to where the trail leaves the road on the right side. Look for the Ptarmigan Trail sign.

From here, follow the trail north, up through a sagebrush meadow. Take a moment along the way to look behind you and appreciate the views of Dillon Reservoir and the Tenmile Range. At the top of the meadow, the trail enters an aspen forest. This section of the trail is particularly beautiful in the fall (mid- to late September). At 1.9 miles (9,876 feet), pass the Anglers Mountain Trail junction sign. At 2.3 miles there is a log bench on your left that makes a good place to take a break.

Continue north along the trail as it gradually contours up and then climbs a series of steep switchbacks to treeline.

Gore Range from Ptarmigan Peak Wilderness.

At 4.2 miles (11,516 feet) arrive at the Ptarmigan Peak Wilderness Area boundary sign. The trail eases somewhat from here as it breaks out of the forest into open alpine meadow. Continue up, northeast now, along this easy trail and enjoy the fantastic views. At 4.7 miles (11,889 feet) you will pass a sign for the Ptarmigan Pass Trail junction. Continue straight on the Ptarmigan Peak Trail. At 5.7 miles (12,481 feet) you will reach a sign on the trail that marks the end of the Ptarmigan Trail and the start of the Ute Peak Trail. Look to your right (east) and you will see a large cairn about 100 yards up that marks the top of Ptarmigan Peak. Follow a weak trail up to the cairn and at 5.7 miles (12,498 feet) reach the summit of Ptarmigan Peak. Enjoy panoramic views in all directions, including the Gore Range, the Tenmile Range, and Dillon Reservoir, all well worth the effort.

To return to the trailhead and the parking area, reverse your route. Take into consideration that, even though it's mostly downhill, you are still 5.8 miles from the trailhead.

PTARMIGAN PEAK 87

# 17. Buffalo Mountain

| | |
|---|---|
| **RATING** | Difficult |
| **ROUND-TRIP DISTANCE** | 5.6 miles |
| **ROUND-TRIP TIME** | 6.0 hours |
| **ELEVATION GAIN** | 3,000 feet |
| **TRAILHEAD** | Buffalo Cabin Trailhead (9,767 feet) (13S 0404742E 4386192N) a.k.a Buffalo Mountain Trailhead |
| **MAPS** | Trails Illustrated 108 Vail, Frisco, Dillon; USGS Vail Pass, USGS Frisco Quadrangles |
| **NEAREST LANDMARK** | Silverthorne |

**OVERVIEW:** A Summit County classic, this hike takes you to the top of 12,777-foot Buffalo Mountain. Immediately west of Silverthorne, Buffalo Mountain is visible from almost anywhere in Silverthorne, Frisco, and Dillon. It's the first mountain you see when you come westbound through the Eisenhower Tunnel. This hike is a steep but gradual climb up the east face of Buffalo along the Buffalo Mountain Trail. The trail includes a challenging section up a steep boulder field that requires careful route finding. Mountain goats are often seen near the summit. The 360-degree views from the top are mind-blowing.

**GETTING THERE:** From Interstate 70 exit 205 (Silverthorne/Dillon), go north on Highway 9 and immediately take a left on Wildernest Road at the first traffic light (Wendy's is on your right). Follow Wildernest Road around the bend for 0.2 mile to a traffic light in front of Lowes. Turn left here to stay on Wildernest Road. Follow Wildernest Road west as it parallels I-70 and then curves right and begins to climb. The name of the road changes to Ryan Gulch Road.

Mountain Goat and Tenmile Range from Buffalo Mountain.

Continue on Ryan Gulch Road for just over 3.0 miles where you will reach the top and see the parking area on your left. This parking area is fairly large but is very popular. Go early. There is no fee to park here. There are no restroom facilities.

**THE ROUTE:** Find the trailhead on the north side of Ryan Gulch Road near the start of the parking area. The trailhead is clearly marked as the Buffalo Cabins Trail. Start by heading north into the forest on this well-worn trail. At about 0.3 mile, pass the Eagles Nest Wilderness Area boundary sign. At about 0.6 mile you will reach a well-marked four-way trail junction. Follow the sign and be sure to go sharp left and stay on the Buffalo Cabins Trail (be careful on the way back too!). At 0.9 mile you will pass the Buffalo Cabin ruins on your right. Imagine spending a winter here. Continue to the left and pass a second cabin at about 1.0 mile (10,373 feet).

After this point, the trail steepens significantly as you begin to switchback up the east flank of Buffalo Mountain on rockier terrain. The trail is clear and easy to follow through this wooded section. At about 1.8 miles (11,440 feet), you will break treeline and enter the bottom of a large boulder field. Continue over to a large and very obvious cairn that marks the trail. Go to the right of this big cairn and pick up the trail on the other side. The trail climbs steeply almost 700 feet up switchbacks that crisscross this boulder field, and it is difficult to follow at times. Try to follow the cairns. If you're going straight up, you're off the trail. Your general direction is up and to the right of the big rock outcrop. At 2.1 miles (11,900 feet) the trail swings right and crosses a vertical rock band. At 2.3 miles (12,100 feet) you will leave the boulder field and pop out on an obvious, easy dirt trail. Be sure to find this point. Congratulations, the hard part is over!

The terrain from this point eases dramatically. Follow the trail as it winds up through low brush and eventually gains the north ridge of Buffalo Mountain. Mountain goats are often seen along this section of the trail. Remember: do not feed or approach them. Continue up the last 200 feet of your climb by picking your way through an easy rock field, and at 2.8 miles, reach the summit at 12,777 feet.

Views from the summit in any direction are spectacular. Immediately to the north is Red Peak (13,189 feet). To the west is South Willow Creek Basin and Red Buffalo Pass (11,700 feet) (Hike 14). To the east is Dillon Reservoir, with the Continental Divide and Grays Peak (14,270 feet) and Torreys Peak (14,267 feet) on the horizon. Keystone Ski Resort is visible in the distance behind the reservoir. To the south, locate Peak 1 (12,805 feet) (Hike 19) and the Tenmile Range. To the southwest is Deming Mountain (12,736 feet), and Mount of the Holy Cross (14,005 feet) is in the distance.

To return to the trailhead and the parking area, reverse your route. Take into consideration that, even though it's mostly downhill, you are 2.8 miles and 3,000 feet of elevation away, and you must also go back down through the boulder field.

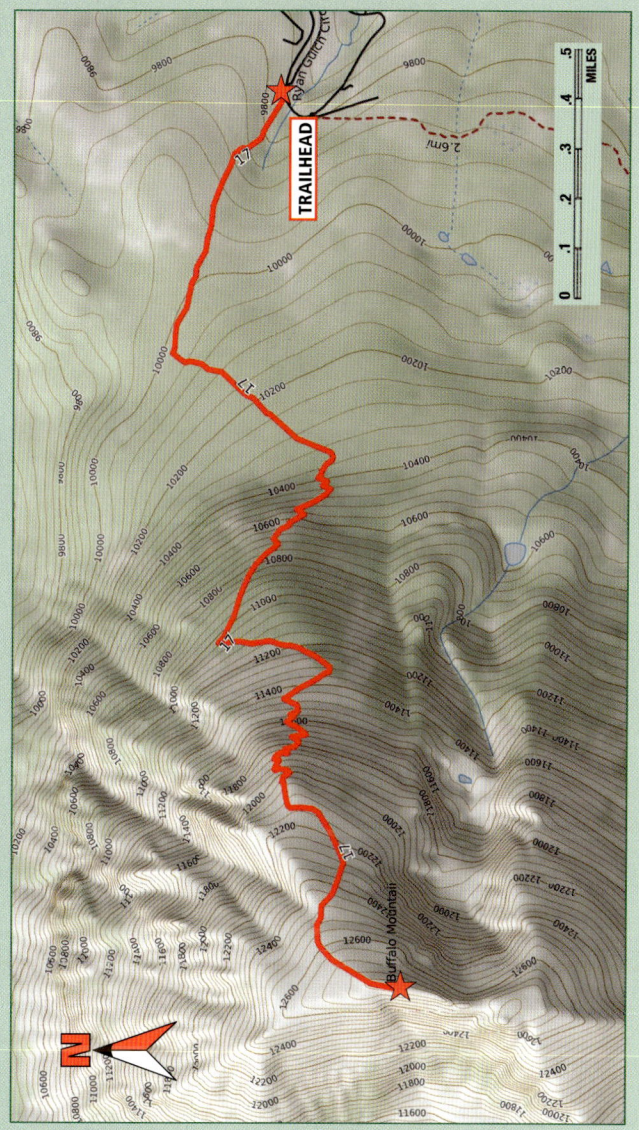

# 18. Colorado Trail—Segment 7

| | |
|---|---|
| **RATING** | Difficult |
| **ROUND-TRIP DISTANCE** | 13.5 miles |
| **ROUND-TRIP TIME** | 8.0 hours |
| **ELEVATION GAIN** | 3,822 feet up; 3,306 feet down |
| **TRAILHEAD** | Gold Hill Trailhead (9,203 feet) (13S 0410423E 4377366N) Wheeler Trailhead (9,764 feet) (13S 0402369E 4372591N) |
| **MAPS** | Trails Illustrated 108 Vail, Frisco, Dillon; Trails Illustrated 109 Breckenridge, Tennessee Pass; USGS Frisco, USGS Breckenridge, USGS Copper Mountain Quadrangles |
| **NEAREST LANDMARK** | Breckenridge (east), Copper Mountain (west) |

**OVERVIEW:** The Colorado Trail is 486 miles long, running from Denver to Durango, and is divided into 33 segments. This hike is segment 7, which runs along the Continental Divide National Scenic Trail. The route includes the entire length of the Gold Hill Trail (north of Breckenridge), a brief section of the Peaks Trail (Hike 9), the entire length of the Miners Creek Trail (up and over the Tenmile Range), and part of the Wheeler National Recreation Trail (down to Copper Mountain). Views of the Tenmile Range, Breckenridge, and Copper Mountain are spectacular. This hike can be broken into shorter outings (as it is in some guide books) but is much more enjoyable to do all in one day. The trails are easy to follow and well marked.

Look for the CT (Colorado Trail) and CDT (Continental Divide Trail) trail markers along the way (see photo).

The route described here goes east to west (Breckenridge to Copper Mountain). It can be done either way. Going east

Colorado Trail along the Tenmile Range

to west requires an additional 500 feet of elevation gain, but the morning light is much better on the east side of the Tenmile Range. This hike requires either a bus ride or a car shuttle back from Copper Mountain (see GETTING THERE).

**GETTING THERE:** Find the Gold Hill Trailhead at the intersection of Highway 9 and Gateway Drive. Gateway Drive is about 0.6 mile north of Tiger Road on Highway 9, north of Breckenridge. The trailhead parking area is next to Highway 9, on the west side. There is no fee to park here. There are no restroom facilities.

Because transportation back from Copper Mountain is required, end the hike at the Summit Stage bus stop in Copper Mountain, at the east end of Copper Road. During the summer months, the bus picks up once an hour (check the schedule). Ride the bus from there to the Frisco bus station, change to the Breckenridge bus, and get off at the Revette Drive stop. Walk 0.25 mile north along the rec path back to the Gold Hill Trailhead.

For a car shuttle back from Copper Mountain, the best place to drop a car is the Far East Lot along Highway 91.

Colorado Trail and Continental Divide Trail Markers.

The Wheeler Trail connects to the rec path immediately east of that lot. Just go left where the Wheeler Trail ends at the rec path and cross the bridge. You're there. Note that this makes the hike about 0.75 mile shorter.

**THE ROUTE:** Find the Gold Hill Trailhead sign next to the kiosks on the west side of the parking area. Head west up the trail over open logged terrain. After about 0.5 mile, stay left at an unmarked fork in the trail and follow some switchbacks before entering the forest. Over the next few miles you will cross some logging roads. Look for the CT/CDT trail markers along the way. At 3.6 miles (9,948 feet) reach the Peaks Trail junction sign. Go left on the Peaks Trail and follow it south for about 0.3 mile. At 3.9 miles (10,020 feet) reach the Miners Creek Trail junction sign. Go right on the Miners Creek Trail and head west again. At 5.2 miles (10,558 feet) pass a four-wheel-drive parking area on your right. Continue west on the Miners Creek Trail and begin to climb toward the Tenmile Range. Just beyond treeline, follow a short set of switchbacks up to a small saddle on the northeast ridge of Peak 5 at 7.0 miles (11,843 feet). Great views of Peaks 1 through 4 are immediately to the north and Breckenridge is to the south.

Continue south on the trail as it contours along the east side of the Tenmile Range. After about a mile, climb up a steep set of switchbacks to where the Miners Creek Trail crests the Tenmile Range between Peaks 5 and 6 at 8.4 miles (12,500 feet). This is the highest point of the hike. Breckenridge Ski Resort is on your left (east) and Copper Mountain Ski Resort is on your right (west). Crystal Peak (13,852 feet) and Pacific Peak (13,950 feet) stand out along the ridge to the south. If the wind isn't bad, this makes a good place to take a break.

From here it's all downhill. Follow the trail south along the ridge for about 0.50 mile before starting to drop down on the west side. At 10.7 miles (11,224 feet) reach the Wheeler Trail junction sign. Take a sharp right onto the Wheeler Trail and head northwest down into the forest. The trail drops 1,500 feet over the next 1.5 miles as it descends

Colorado Trail and Continental Divide Trail sign.

Colorado Trail along the Tenmile Range.

toward Copper Mountain. At 12.7 miles (9,764 feet) the trail reaches the rec path sign. If you dropped a car at the Far East Lot, go left across the bridge and into that lot. Otherwise, watch for bikes and follow the rec path north for just over 0.50 mile to a three-way intersection. Go left and cross a bridge before reaching a traffic intersection on Highway 91. Cross the highway and find the bus stop immediately to your right on the north side of Copper Road.

COLORADO TRAIL—SEGMENT 7

# 19. Peak 1

| RATING | Difficult |
| --- | --- |
| ROUND-TRIP DISTANCE | 7.2 miles |
| ROUND-TRIP TIME | 8.0 hours |
| ELEVATION GAIN | 3,700 feet |
| TRAILHEAD | Interstate 70 Exit 201 Parking Area (9,121 feet) (13S 0404583E 4381156N) |
| MAPS | Trails Illustrated 108 Vail, Frisco, Dillon; USGS Frisco Quadrangle |
| NEAREST LANDMARK | Frisco |
| OPTIONS | Mount Royal (10,502 feet) Mount Victoria (11,785 feet) |

**OVERVIEW:** This is probably the most technical hike in this book. Towering over Frisco, Peak 1 (12,805 feet) is the iconic mountain at the north end of the Tenmile Range. A difficult day hike, the 360-degree views from the top are well worth the effort. If you are in good shape and comfortable with short, unexposed easy class 3 scrambling, this hike is for you. Start early and make sure the weather is favorable. It is not possible to see weather coming from the southwest until you are high on the summit ridge.

For a shorter day, consider Mt. Royal (10,502 feet) or Mt. Victoria (11,785 feet) as a destination (see OPTIONS). Both are much less challenging.

These trails are not recommended for winter travel, due to avalanche danger, and may not be clear of snow and ice until July.

**GETTING THERE:** Parking for this hike is at the west end of Main Street in Frisco, immediately *east* of I-70 (exit 201). Don't confuse this parking area with the parking area for

Frisco and Dillon Reservoir from Peak 1.

North Tenmile Creek (Hike 7), which is on the other side of I-70. This is a relatively large parking area. There is no fee to park here. There are restroom facilities.

**THE ROUTE:** Find the paved trail on the southeast corner of the parking area, near the kiosk. Follow the trail across Tenmile Creek on a large bridge to an intersection with the rec path. Follow the paved rec path to a triangular intersection. Go left at the intersection and continue southeast along the rec path for another 0.25 mile. Always walk on the right side of the rec path and watch for bikes (see rec path rules on page 12). At 0.4 mile (9,124 feet), you will reach the Mt. Royal Trailhead. Leave the rec path and follow the obvious dirt trail up to the right. You will pass two unmarked forks in the trail. Stay right both times and continue up. At 0.9 mile (9,518 feet) you will come to the Masontown settlement ruins. Masontown was a late 19th century mining settlement, the remains of which were destroyed by an avalanche in 1926.

After Masontown, the trail steepens significantly up a switchback and long straightaway. At 1.6 miles (10,295 feet) reach the well-marked Mt. Royal Trail junction. If your goal for the day is Mt. Royal, take this trail to the right. Otherwise, continue up toward Mt. Victoria and Peak 1. At just over 10,600 feet, the trail finally reaches the north ridge of Peak 1. Follow the trail along the ridge and at 2.6 miles (11,600 feet) arrive at the communication towers below Mt. Victoria. Go another 0.2 mile up where you will break treeline, and at 2.8 miles (11,785 feet), reach Mt. Victoria.

Peak 1 is now clearly visible to the south. While the general direction remains clear, the trail is sometimes harder to follow as it crosses rocky sections along the ridge. At 3.5 miles (12,585 feet) you will reach a prominent notch in the ridge, about 250 feet below the summit. Study the remaining route before you. Start on the west side of the ridge and make your way up through this rocky section. Some cairns mark the trail but you must pick your way through most of it. At about 80 feet below the summit, cross the ridge and drop slightly to the east where easier terrain leads to the top. At 3.6 miles reach the summit of Peak 1 (12,805 feet). Enjoy panoramic views in all directions: north to the Gore Range, northeast to Frisco and the Dillon Reservoir, south along the Tenmile Range, southwest to Copper Mountain Ski Resort, and west to Uneva Peak (12,522 feet).

To return to the trailhead and the parking area, reverse your route. Take into consideration that you are 3.6 miles from the parking area and 3,700 feet above it.

## OPTIONS

**MT. ROYAL (10,502 FEET):** Total round-trip from the trailhead: 4.0 miles; 1,415 feet gain.

For an easier day, take the Mt. Royal Trail spur. Follow this trail up an additional 0.4 mile (and 200 feet) to where it levels out and the views to the north open up. I-70 is visible 1,400 feet below. Continue northeast along the ridge to the high point for the best views. To return to the parking area, reverse your route. Do not attempt to downclimb the northeast side of Mt. Royal.

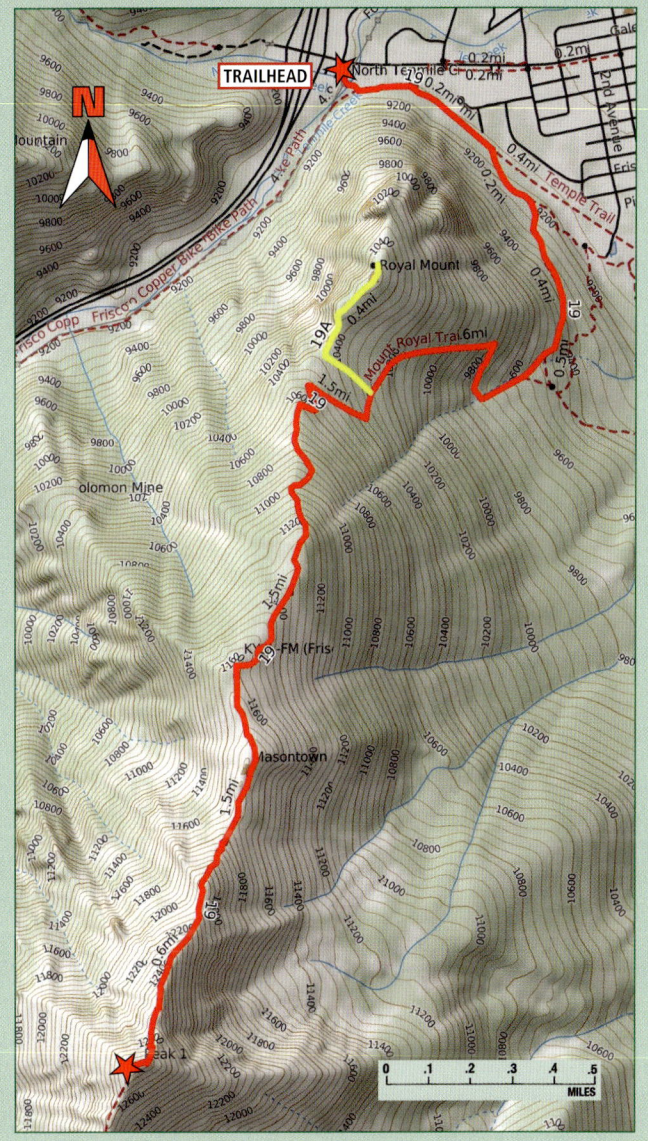

PEAK 1 101

# 20. Quandary Peak

| RATING | Difficult |
|---|---|
| ROUND-TRIP DISTANCE | 6.2 miles |
| ROUND-TRIP TIME | 6.0 hours |
| ELEVATION GAIN | 3,310 feet |
| TRAILHEAD | Quandary Peak Trailhead (10,922 feet) (13S 0408545E 4360099N) |
| MAPS | Trails Illustrated 109 Breckenridge, Tennessee Pass; USGS Breckenridge Quadrangle |
| NEAREST LANDMARK | Blue River |

**OVERVIEW:** Quandary Peak is the only 14,000-foot peak wholly contained within the borders of Summit County. This hike follows the standard route up the east ridge to the summit (14,265 feet). Quandary is considered one of the easiest 14ers to climb, but it is strenuous—much like walking up a three-mile staircase. Because of its popularity, the trail is busy during the summer months, especially on weekends. If you have not climbed a Colorado 14er, this is a good place to start. The views from the top are well worth the effort.

Be sure to take extra layers. It can be *much* cooler at the summit than at the trailhead. Also, most of this hike is above treeline, with limited visibility to the west. Approaching storms may be difficult to detect. The general rule is start early and plan to be off the top by noon.

Winter travel along this route is beyond the scope of this book and not recommended unless you have alpine climbing experience.

**GETTING THERE:** From the intersection of Highway 9 and Boreas Pass Road on the south side of Breckenridge, head

East Ridge of Quandary Peak from Hoosier Pass.

south on Highway 9 for about 7.3 miles, through the town of Blue River. Look for the street sign and turn right on Blue Lakes Road (FDR 850). You will immediately see a big parking area on your right. This is the overflow parking area for the Quandary Peak Trail. Go past this parking area and immediately turn right on McCullough Gulch Road (FDR 851). Follow McCullough Gulch Road for 0.2 mile to a small trailhead parking area on your right. If this parking area is full, either park along the road or return to the overflow parking area. If you park along the road, be sure not to block private property access. There is no fee to park. There are no restroom facilities.

**THE ROUTE:** Find the Quandary Peak Trailhead on McCullough Gulch Road, across from the small parking area. Follow this well-traveled trail northwest up into the forest. Cross some old mining roads early and be sure to pick up the trail again on the other side. At 0.8 mile (11,620 feet) the trail crosses a flatter section before contouring over to and along the south side of the east ridge, now above treeline. A series of switchbacks over well-maintained trail will take you up to the east ridge proper. At mile 2.3 (13,140 feet) the trail along the ridge eases briefly at the bottom of Quandary's massive east face. The view of the remaining route to the summit is before you. Look for mountain goats along this stretch.

Monte Cristo Valley and Wheeler Mountain from the Quandary Trail.

Once across this flatter section, begin the final push to the summit. The remaining trail is sometimes indistinct but the objective is not. Stay on the ridge and look for cairns along the way. At just over 14,000 feet, the trail eases as you finally approach the top. Walk a short distance from there and at 3.1 miles (14,265 feet) arrive at the summit.

Enjoy panoramic views in all directions. Upper McCullough Gulch (Hike 5) is the broad valley at the base of Quandary's north face, with Pacific Peak (13,951 feet) at the northwest corner. The Tenmile Range is to the north. Mt. Lincoln (14,286 feet) and the Mosquito Range are directly to the south. Mt. Elbert (14,433 feet) and Mt. Massive (14,421 feet), in the Sawatch Range, are visible far to the southwest. Holy Cross Wilderness and Mt. of the Holy Cross (14,005 feet) are on the horizon to the west.

To return to the trailhead and the parking area, reverse your route. Take into consideration that you are 3.1 miles from the trailhead and 3,310 feet above it. Because the trail is rocky, the descent can take almost as long as the ascent.

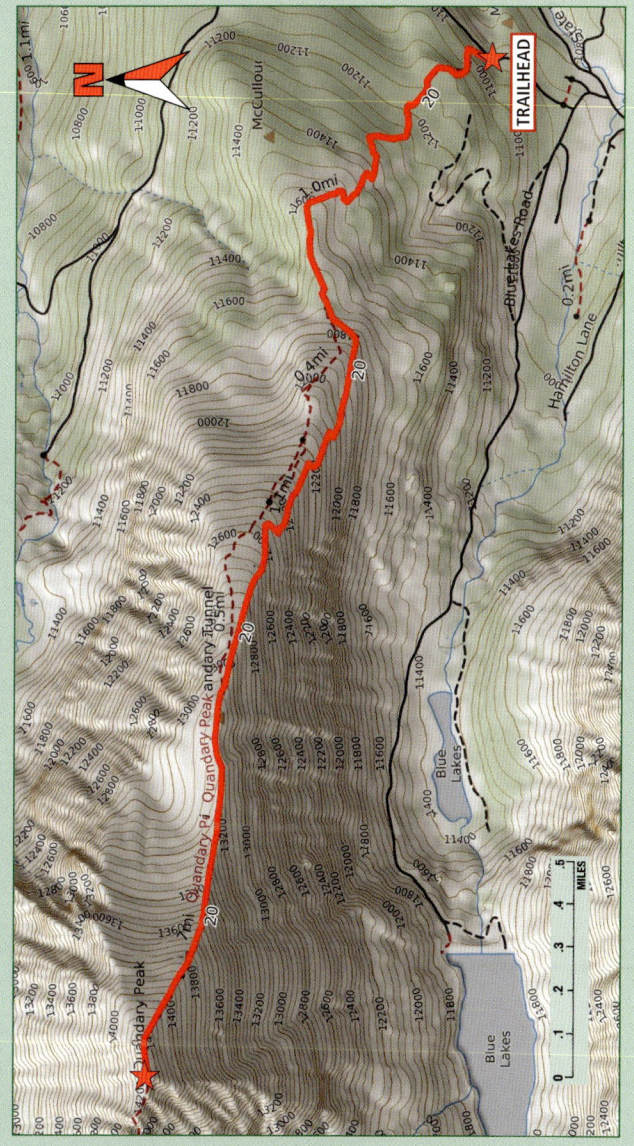

## About the Author

Marshall Hull lives in Summit County, Colorado with his wife Emiko. They are both year-round outdoor enthusiasts. Marshall is an expert at backcountry navigation and GPS tracking. He is also a part-time instructor for the Colorado Mountain Club.

# Checklist

## THE BEST SUMMIT COUNTY HIKES

| | | | |
|---|---|---|---|
| ☐ | HIKE 1 | Black Powder Pass | 16 |
| ☐ | HIKE 2 | Lower Cataract Lake | 20 |
| ☐ | HIKE 3 | Lily Pad Lake | 24 |
| ☐ | HIKE 4 | Mayflower Gulch | 30 |
| ☐ | HIKE 5 | McCullough Gulch | 34 |
| ☐ | HIKE 6 | Shrine Mountain | 38 |
| ☐ | HIKE 7 | North Tenmile Creek | 42 |
| ☐ | HIKE 8 | Continental Divide Overlook | 46 |
| ☐ | HIKE 9 | Peaks Trail | 50 |
| ☐ | HIKE 10 | Mohawk Lakes | 56 |
| ☐ | HIKE 11 | Argentine Pass | 62 |
| ☐ | HIKE 12 | Eccles Pass | 66 |
| ☐ | HIKE 13 | Uneva Pass | 70 |
| ☐ | HIKE 14 | Red Buffalo Pass | 74 |
| ☐ | HIKE 15 | Willow Lakes | 80 |
| ☐ | HIKE 16 | Ptarmigan Peak | 84 |
| ☐ | HIKE 17 | Buffalo Mountain | 88 |
| ☐ | HIKE 18 | Colorado Trail Section 7 | 92 |
| ☐ | HIKE 19 | Peak 1 | 98 |
| ☐ | HIKE 20 | Quandary Peak | 102 |

Illustration by Jesse Crock

# Join Today.
# Adventure Tomorrow.

The Colorado Mountain Club helps you maximize living in an outdoor playground and connects you with other adventure-loving mountaineers. We summit 14ers, climbs rock faces, work to protect the mountain experience and educate generations of Coloradans.

**Visit cmc.org/readerspecials**
for great membership offers to our readers.